DRIVER'S RECEIPT

I acknowledge receipt of the School Bus Driver's Safety Handbook, which covers the following safety topics:

Passenger Safety

Special Needs Passengers

Driving Techniques

Defensive Driving and Emergency Maneuvers

Speed and Space Management

Seeing Hazards

Breakdowns and Accidents

Extreme Weather

Compliance

Personal Health Issues

D0946281

_____

Driver's Signature   Date

_____

Company

_____

Company Supervisor's Signature

NOTE: This receipt shall be read and signed by the driver. A responsible company supervisor shall countersign the receipt and place in the driver's training file.

Keller's
School Bus
Driver's
Safety
Handbook

©2001
J. J. Keller & Associates, Inc.
3003 W. Breezewood Lane, P. O. Box 368
Neenah, Wisconsin 54957-0368
Phone: (920) 722-2848
www.jjkeller.com

Library of Congress Catalog Card Number:
2001088075

ISBN 1-57943-962-4

Canadian Goods and Services Tax (GST)
Number: R123-317687

Printed in the U.S.A.

First Edition, First Printing, April 2001

Table of Contents

Introduction

As a school bus driver, have you ever contemplated what a unique job you've chosen? After all, there is no other occupation that combines looking out for the well-being of children with the responsibilities of driving some of the largest vehicles on the road. Semi-drivers, passenger bus drivers, day-care workers, teachers — none of them do quite what you do.

Because your job is unique, we've written a unique book for you. *Keller's School Bus Driver's Safety Handbook* covers the wide array of skills you need to do your job well and keep your passengers safe. This book addresses such things as passenger safety, how to establish a good rapport with your students, disciplinary situations, and transporting special needs students. It also covers the essential skills you need to drive your large vehicle: defensive driving principles, evasive maneuver techniques, how to see hazards, and speed and space management. Additional topics include complying with federal and state regulations and how to keep your own personal health in tip-top shape so you can be the safest driver possible.

You may encounter this book as part of the training at your company or school. We know it will provide an excellent introduction to the career path you've chosen. After training, hang on to the book as a convenient reference.

Happy and safe driving!

Passenger Safety

Many people drive a vehicle for a living, but nobody has more precious cargo than you do: children. However, while your cargo is precious, it can also be very challenging. Children are often impulsive, noisy, unpredictable, and may challenge your authority.

In order to transport your charges safely, you must have clear rules and procedures and enforce them firmly and consistently. Your rules should cover how your passengers enter and exit your school bus and how they behave while riding. However, remember what we said — children are unpredictable. Beyond the rules, you must also take extra precautions to make sure your passengers enter, exit, and ride safely.

This chapter will primarily focus on entering and exiting procedures (including the "Danger Zone"), student conduct on the bus, and ways you can manage student behavior.

Entering and Exiting the School Bus

Getting on and off the school bus is the most dangerous part of the whole school bus trip. According to the National Highway Transportation Safety Administration, three times as many children are fatally injured while getting on or off a school bus as are killed while actually riding on a bus.

Safe loading and unloading requires using an established procedure you and your students understand. It also requires your vigilant attention to make sure each child gets on and off the bus safely.

The following sections detail how your students should enter and exit your bus.

Entering procedures

- As you approach your students' pick-up point, **turn on your warning lights** about 100 feet before making your stop.

- Slowly and carefully come to a **stop in the farthest right traffic lane** of the road. If the students are waiting on the right side of the road, stop at a point where you can still see the children — make them walk to your bus so you can keep them in your sight as long as possible.

- **Activate the stop arm** after you've stopped but before you open the door.

- **Scan** all around your bus **and check your mirrors** for traffic to make sure it is stopped in all directions.

- If the traffic is stopped and it's safe for your passengers, **open the door.**

- If your students are crossing the street or road, give them a **signal** that it is safe to cross. This signal could be a nod or hand gesture, but make sure your students know what the signal is ahead of time and that they are not to cross until you give the signal. (Don't use a wave as a signal — a motorist could misinterpret it and think you are giving them permission to pass you.) Students who cross the street should always walk 10 feet in front of the bus so you can see them.

- **Count** the students at the stop and count them again as they get on your bus. If any student is missing, DON'T MOVE THE BUS. Shut off the bus and get out, if necessary, to find the missing student.

- **Look** around the bus, **check** your mirrors, and **listen** for any last-second signs that a student could be near the bus and in danger. A late student could be hurrying toward your bus or a parent may be trying to get your attention because he/she sees something you don't.

- Retract your stop arm and turn off the warning lights.

- **Check your mirrors** one more time, make sure all the **students are seated**, and **proceed** when the traffic allows.

The Danger Zone

An important concept to understand — for you and your students — is the school bus's "Danger Zone."

The Danger Zone is an area 10 feet in front of, behind, and on each side of the school bus. When students or vehicles are in the bus's Danger Zone, you cannot see them. This extremely dangerous area is where many of the accidents involving buses occur.

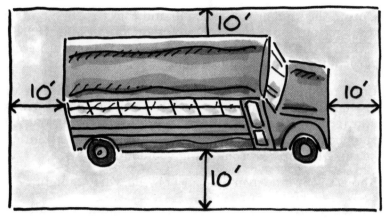

- **In front of the bus.** Students should always cross at least 10 feet (that's five "giant steps" for your younger passengers) in front of the bus. Tell your students that they should be far enough away from the bus that they can see your face — they need to see you so you can see them.

- **Behind the bus.** Students should NEVER cross behind your bus because you will not be able to see them. As many as three or four small vehicles can be in this blind spot without your awareness. This is one of the reasons you should never back your bus unless absolutely necessary.

- **Your right side.** It's possible for students or small vehicles to be right near your service door and be completely invisible to you. Do not let students "hang out" near the bus when it is parked — they should always be at least 10 feet away when they are not immediately entering or exiting the bus.

- **Your left side.** Students and vehicles can be out of the range of your driver's side mirror and peripheral vision on your left side as well. As with all your blind spots, keep a watchful eye on this area.

As the driver, you need to be constantly vigilant for children and vehicles that may be in the Danger Zone. Your students need to be educated (and probably continually reminded) about the importance of staying out of this area.

On the bus

Once your students are on the bus, they should take their seats quickly and orderly. Unless standees are allowed in your state and school district, all students should be seated before you move the bus. To limit injuries in front- and rear-end collisions, the National Transportation Safety Board recommends that students do not sit in the front or rearmost rows of passenger seats unless all other seats are occupied.

The maximum capacity of a school bus is designated by the bus's manufacturer. Realize, however, that these capacities are usually calculated based on elementary-aged children. If you transport many high school or middle school students, you will not be able to load as many passengers on your bus. Follow your company or school district policy in regard to pupil capacity. If you find your bus is overcrowded, you should let your supervisor know so the problem can be dealt with.

Emergency exits should be kept unobstructed at all times. Make sure book bags, band instruments, and other items are not spilling into the aisles or blocking the exits.

Exiting procedures

Exiting the bus presents the same dangers as entering the bus. To get your students off the bus safely, follow these procedures:

- **Turn on your warning lights** about 100 feet before stopping for drop-off.

- Slowly and carefully come to a **stop in the farthest right traffic lane** of the road. Students should stay seated until you come to a complete stop.

- **Activate the stop arm** after you've stopped but before you open the door.

- **Scan** all around your bus **and check your mirrors** for traffic to make sure it is stopped in all directions. Do not open your door until you are sure the situation is completely safe for your exiting passengers.

- **Count the students** getting off at this stop and then **open the door.**

- **Count each student** who gets off the bus. Students should get far away enough from the bus so that you can see all of them.

- Students who have to cross the road should **get 10 feet in front of your bus** and wait for your signal.

- **Check you mirrors and scan traffic.** When the situation is safe, give your students a **signal** to cross.

- **Re-count** all the students to make sure everyone has gotten off and gotten away from the bus safely. If any student is missing, DON'T MOVE THE BUS. Shut off the bus and get out, if necessary, to find the missing student.

- **Look** around the bus, **check** your mirrors, and **listen** for any last-second signs that a student could be near the bus and in danger.

- Retract your stop arm and turn off the warning lights.

- **Check your mirrors** one more time and **proceed** when the traffic allows.

Additional notes on entering and exiting the bus

Here are some additional things to think about regarding the loading and unloading process:

- **Give entering and exiting students your full attention.** As we said, entering and exiting the school bus is the most dangerous part of your students' trips. If other students are being rowdy or there are discipline issues you need to attend to, do it after your passengers are safely loaded. Don't let the other students distract you during this critical procedure. Have entering students immediately take their seats in an orderly fashion so you can concentrate on the rest of the students entering the bus.

- **Use consistent signals and have a warning signal.** Be consistent in how you signal students to cross the street. Also, don't signal in a way that could make stopped motorists think you are giving them the okay to pass your bus. In addition to your crossing signal, have a warning signal — perhaps a special honk of your horn — that will tell students to get back to their bus stop location in case a traffic situation suddenly develops that puts your passengers in danger. Ideally, all the school bus drivers in your company should use the same signals.

- **Watch for students with loose papers.** Loose papers or other items that are easily dropped may cause a child to stop in your blind spots or even send an unthinking child scurrying under your bus to retrieve a lost item. Instruct your passengers to never stop to retrieve something they've dropped when getting on or off the bus. Have them get on the bus and tell you about the lost item. As the  driver, however, stay alert when you see children with loose papers — in a panic over lost homework, they may not remember to follow your instructions.

- **Watch out for students with drawstrings, loose clothing, or backpacks.** Drawstrings in clothing, scarves, loose clothes, and backpack straps have been known to get caught in a bus's handrail or door. Tragedy has resulted when these children were dragged to their deaths by unknowing drivers. Be extra alert when you see kids with these items and always  remember to never move your bus until you can see all the exiting children are safely off and away from the vehicle.

- **Report poor pick-up and drop-off points to your supervisor.** A good loading or unloading spot is one where other motorists can see your bus and the entering/exiting children in plenty of time to safely stop. If you think a designated loading or unloading spot is dangerous, notify your supervisor. Perhaps a more suitable spot can be found.

Passenger Conduct

To transport your children safely, you need to be able to concentrate on your driving and the critical tasks of loading and unloading your passengers. It's important that the behavior of your students doesn't distract you from those important tasks. Clear expectations for passenger conduct, explained up front at the beginning of the school year, will help you maintain an orderly and safe bus for all your students.

Most school districts have established rules governing bus conduct. Some conduct, of course, is never acceptable: violence, vandalism, or the bringing of weapons, drugs, or alcohol onto the bus are not only going to be a violation of conduct rules, they could also lead to police involvement.

The rules for passenger conduct should be designed to help you transport your students efficiently and safely. A typical set of conduct rules could read:

- Students should arrive at their pick-up point five minutes before the bus is scheduled to arrive.

- Students who must cross the street to board the bus should walk 10 feet in front of the bus and only cross the street when the driver signals to do so.

- Passengers should immediately take their seats when they get on the bus and remain seated while the bus is in motion.

- All books, bags, instruments, and other student items should be kept out of the bus aisles.

- Students may talk quietly amongst themselves. Screaming, yelling, or swearing is not allowed.

- Students must keep arms, legs, heads, books, bags, and other items inside the bus at all times.

- Students must clean up after themselves. Littering is not allowed.

- All students should treat their fellow passengers and the bus driver with respect.

- Students must obey the directions of the bus driver.

Your school district or bus company may have additional rules about food or gum on the bus, assigned seats, radios, or any number of other issues. Or you may be able to set some of these rules yourself for your own bus. Whatever the case, rules are most effective if you discuss them with your students up front and explain they are for the safety and comfort of all the passengers on the bus. Even young children give more respect to rules when they understand there is a purpose behind them.

Another good idea is to have students take a written copy of the rules home to be signed and returned by their parents. Getting the parents involved ensures that everyone involved in the students' transportation understands conduct expectations.

Managing Student Behavior

While conduct rules may be set by your company or school district, enforcing the rules and managing student behavior is a day-to-day challenge left to you. While managing student behavior can be one of the most challenging aspects of your job, it cannot be ignored — you must maintain control of your bus to operate it safely.

Establishing a good relationship

You will have an easier time getting your students to behave if you establish a good relationship with them from the beginning.

How do you establish a good relationship? Be friendly with your students. Smile when they get on board and greet them by name. Take an interest in them: admire a second-grader's new book bag, or wish a high school student good luck at her upcoming track meet. Let your attitude set a positive tone for your relationship with the students.

And while you are trying to manage student behavior, don't forget about positive reinforcement. Praise your students for behaving on the bus. If you've had particular trouble with certain students, make extra sure you let them know when they are behaving well and that you appreciate their cooperation. Many times students act up for attention, so make positive attention their goal instead of negative attention. You might also try giving out treats, stickers, pencils, or other small items as a reward for good behavior.

Remember, being friendly doesn't mean being a pushover — enforcing rules appropriately is still important. But if you can establish a relationship where the students both respect you and like you, they are less likely to act up and give you problems in the discipline department.

Discipline situations

While you may work hard to establish a good relationship with your students, kids are kids and some episodes of misbehavior are almost inevitable. When disciplinary problems arise, follow these principles to get the situation under control:

- **Don't argue and don't get angry.** You are the adult and you are in charge of the bus. Don't get drawn into an argument or let students push your emotional buttons. Handle disciplinary situations calmly and firmly.

- **Be consistent.** Children will not understand if a certain behavior is acceptable one day and not the next. Also, be consistent in how you treat each student — don't play favorites.

- **Do what you say you will.** Kids can smell an idle threat. If you threaten to take some type of disciplinary action, make sure your school's policies allow you to do it and then follow through. If you don't follow through, your credibility among your students will take a huge nosedive.

- **Nip problems early.** Don't let a situation get out of control before you deal with it. Talk to the student early and remind him/her what the behavior standards are.

- **Discipline individuals.** If one student is causing the problems, deal with the ringleader. Don't punish a whole group of students for the actions of one.

Stopping the bus

There may be occasions when a problem gets so serious that it's a safety threat to the other students or keeps your from concentrating on your driving. If this situation occurs, you need to stop the bus to handle the problem.

Get the bus safely off the roadway, turn off the ignition, and take out the key. Deal with the student(s) and the behavior problem. You may need to separate students or move one or more to the front of the bus where you can keep a closer eye on them. As always, handle the situation calmly and don't threaten something you can't or won't do.

Extreme discipline situations

While it would be nice to pretend that you will never encounter discipline situations beyond spit balls, graffiti, or general rowdiness, that may not be realistic in this day and age. School violence is a huge concern and isn't just confined to the school walls. Another troubling problem is sexual harassment lawsuits based on student-to-student actions that occurred on school buses. Hopefully, your school district has detailed policies on how to deal with these issues, but some general guidelines follow:

Violence. In a situation where a student threatens violence or to bring a weapon on the bus, report it as soon as possible to your supervisor. Many districts have adopted zero-tolerance policies that require the reporting of even seemingly far-fetched threats. If a serious fight breaks out while on your bus, you should, of course, try to stop it and prevent anyone from being injured. If you are unable to stop the fight, try to get the other students out of danger's way and call the police on a cell phone or radio your company/school to make the call.

Sexual conduct. When conduct or student comments become sexual in nature, it can be hard to know how to react. While you may observe conduct that is unequivocally unacceptable, oftentimes the line between pre-pubescent teasing and sexual harassment can seem gray. In general, if you notice behavior that is questionable — lewd comments directed from one student to another, or touching that could be sexual in nature — separate the students, explain to them that the behavior is unacceptable, report the incident to your supervisor, and follow your district's policies.

Following Disciplinary Policies and Procedures

Your school district or bus company should have specific policies and procedures for dealing with disciplinary problems. Many times these involve reporting offenders to their parents or school officials. In cases of serious or repeated violations of conduct rules, students might have their bus riding privileges suspended or even revoked.

As the driver, it is important for you to understand and follow the established policies governing discipline and your interaction with your students. Going beyond these policies and procedures could have serious legal consequences for you, your school, and/or your bus company.

Unacceptable discipline techniques

Some means of discipline — which were sometimes allowed in decades past — are simply not acceptable today.

Physical contact. Physical discipline, such as spanking a child or physically forcing a student to sit in his/her seat, is going to be unacceptable in most school districts. In general, unless you need to physically break up a fight or defend yourself, you should not have any physical contact with a student.

Putting a student off the bus. When a student has been repeatedly violating the rules and creating a disturbance on the bus, you could be tempted to make him/her immediately get off the bus and walk the rest of the way home or to school. Don't do it. Making the student walk could put him/her in danger and, if there is an accident, you, the school district, and/or the bus company could be held liable. If you want the student off your bus, follow your company's/school's procedures for suspending the student's privilege to ride.

Verbal abuse. Although there may be times you become angry with misbehaving students, don't become verbally abusive. You can be critical of students' behavior and express your displeasure, but do not call the students names (like "stupid"), swear, or ever use racial/ethnic slurs. A parental complaint that you've been verbally abusive could cost you your job or even evolve into a lawsuit.

Sexual contact

While you never want to do anything to a student that could be seen as physical abuse, you also want to be cautious of any actions toward a student that could be perceived as sexual. Obviously, sexual conduct with a student of any age is completely unacceptable, but your school/company may have additional policies to protect you and them against sexual misconduct allegations. While it may be your totally innocent instinct to give a hug to a young child upset about a bad test or other problem, it may not be acceptable where you work.

Know your company's/district's policies about what is and isn't allowed and always think about how your actions will be perceived before you touch a student.

Using Seat Belts

Currently, most states, school districts, and school bus companies have rejected putting seat belts in large school buses. Instead of using seat belts, crash protection is provided through a concept called "compartmententalization." In compartmentalization, passengers are protected by the closely spaced seats that have large, energy-absorbing seat backs.

However, belts are required on smaller school buses (those weighing 10,000 pounds or less) because government regulators have decided these vehicles bear more of a resemblance to passenger vehicles than large school busses. Individual localities are also free to put seat belts on any size school bus if they believe it provides a safety benefit.

While the benefits of seat belt usage on school buses is an issue of some controversy, it's unequivocal that seat belts must be used properly to be effective. If your company/district requires your students to wear seat belts, be familiar with the policy and the proper wearing of the belts.

End of the Trip

When you've finished your morning or afternoon trip, and all of your students have been safely delivered to school or their homes, you have one more critical task to perform: inspecting your bus.

Walk down the aisles and look in each and every seat. There have been several occurrences of children falling asleep on the bus and failing to get off at their designated stop. Curled up on a bus seat, they can be invisible to you unless you make a point of inspecting the bus. The consequences of leaving a child on the bus are very serious: frightening the child, endangering the child's safety (particularly in very hot or cold weather), panicking the student's parents, possible lawsuits, bad publicity, and potential job termination for you. Don't forget this task!

Inspecting the bus at the end of the day also gives you a chance to clean up any litter and make note of any damages to the interior of the bus. Your company or district may require you to do a mechanical inspection of the bus at the end of your trip as well.

— Notes —

Driver _____

Instructor _____

Date _____

Location _____

Passenger Safety Review

1. The most dangerous part of the school bus ride is:
    a. The morning ride to school
    b. The afternoon ride home
    c. Getting on and off the bus
    d. Field trips

2. When your bus is stopped and you are about to load your passengers, you should:
    a. Scan around the bus and check your mirrors
    b. Give students crossing the street a pre-determined signal that the traffic is clear
    c. Count the students waiting and count them again as they get on the bus
    d. All of the above

3. The Danger Zone is a blind area 10 feet in front, in back, and on each side of the school bus.
    a. True
    b. False

4. You should be extra alert when you see a student wearing a loose scarf or drawstring clothing because these items can get caught in the bus handrail or door.
    a. True
    b. False

5. The primary reason for having conduct rules for your passengers is to:
    a. Teach children discipline
    b. Keep the bus clean
    c. Allow you to concentrate on driving safely
    d. Keep the bus perfectly quiet

6. Establishing a positive relationship with your students won't help you maintain discipline.
   a. True
   b. False

7. Idle threats are a good way to discipline children.
   a. True
   b. False

8. If a serious discipline situation breaks out, you should:
   a. Yell at the students while you are driving down the road
   b. Stop the bus and deal with the situation
   c. Shove the student who is creating the disturbance
   d. Make the offending students get off the bus and walk the rest of the way to school

9. Seat belts are required in all school buses.
   a. True
   b. False

10. The most important reason for inspecting the bus at the end of your trip is:
    a. To pick up litter
    b. To make note of any torn seats
    c. To find books left behind by students
    d. To find any child who may still be on the bus

Special Needs Passengers

Driving a school bus is a unique and demanding job under typical circumstances, but a driver who transports special needs passengers has even more responsibilities and issues to consider. While transporting special needs passengers requires more work on the driver's part, many drivers who transport these children describe their jobs as extremely rewarding and prefer special needs routes.

What does "special needs" mean? A special needs student could be a child with a mental disability, a physical disability, a behavior disorder, or a health condition that requires special care. Addressing the transportation needs of these students will require a team effort involving parents, school personnel, the bus company, and you.

While there are many issues in transporting special needs children (and the issues change with each unique child and situation), this chapter will talk about some general concerns in special needs transportation and then address some specific issues about transporting passengers who use wheeled mobility devices.

Managing and Interacting with Special Needs Students

Above everything else, the kids you transport are kids, and you should treat them that way. Don't let your interest and efforts in dealing with their disability or condition become the focus of your relationship with them. Your students are kids first, then kids with disabilities.

Much of the material in this chapter, particularly the portions dealing with WMDs and vehicle lifts, was used with permission from the Iowa Department of Education.

Communication. Learn about the individuals on your bus and how to communicate with each student. Take time to listen and pay attention to each child. While some students may have communication barriers, take care not to "talk down" to any student, but especially students whose disabilities are purely physical — talk to these kids as you would any other child their age.

Independence. Learning to function in the world is part of the education of a special needs student, so allow your passengers as much independence as they can safely handle. When possible, let them do things for themselves rather than doing the tasks for them. Allowing your students the freedom and opportunity to make choices while learning to be safe on the bus will help them develop independent attitudes.

Communication Issues

With special needs students, it is probably even more critical that you maintain good communication with parents and school officials on issues affecting your passengers. Whenever a student starts bus transportation, it's a good idea to have a meeting among the parents, school officials, bus personnel, and the driver. During the meeting, the participants can discuss:

- The unique needs of the child, including physical and medical needs.

- Any medical or behavioral issues the driver should be aware of.

- The school district's transportation policies and procedures.

- Special concerns regarding the route or vehicle equipment.

- Parental ideas on how to make the ride positive for the student.

Having such a meeting will allow you, the driver, to get first-hand knowledge about the child and establish an open and positive communication with the parents.

During the year, you should keep parents and school officials informed about your students' good days and behavior, and any special or unusual problems you may be having. Tell them the facts with specific examples. In turn, parents and teachers can give you insight into the issues they are encountering with the child. If you are aware of problems in the classroom, you may be able to reinforce the teacher's efforts while the child is on the bus. You may also be able to provide the teachers with information that will be useful in further planning for the student.

Transporting Students Using WMDs

Students with disabilities use a variety of devices to meet mobility needs, including manual wheelchairs, power wheelchairs, scooters, carts, gurneys, strollers, and tricycles. Because of the variety of devices, the preferred term is becoming "wheeled mobility device" (rather than "wheelchair") for these items.

When you transport a student with a WMD, you need to become familiar with the equipment the student uses. You will need to know:

- Where the brakes are and how to engage and disengage them.

- How to turn a powered WMD on and off.

- Which accessories (e.g. lap trays, computers, communication devices, crutches) need to be removed during loading, unloading and transit; how to remove and replace them; and where and how to secure them during transit.

- How to steer or maneuver the device up and down curbs, ramps, on and off the lift, and inside the vehicle.

- Who will maneuver the device — you or the student.

- The points on the WMD frame to which the tie-downs should be attached.

Securing WMDs in the school bus

Students who can be transferred to a vehicle seat or will fit into a child safety seat should ride in those seats rather than the WMD, if practical. Vehicle and child safety seats have been tested to meet Federal Motor Vehicle Safety Standards and are the best choice if they fit the individual student's needs.

If the student must remain in the WMD during transport, it should be a device the manufacturer has recommended for use in vehicles and it should be in good repair for transport.

You should become familiar with the instructions from the WMD manufacturer on transporting the device and the directions for using the WMD securement system in your bus. However, following are some general guidelines for securing WMDs:

- The WMD and the occupant should face the front of the vehicle.

- Center the WMD between the floor track or plates. Position the WMD so there will be a 45 degree angle from the floor tracks or plates to where the straps attach to the WMD frame.

- Apply the handbrakes on the WMD or turn off the power if the WMD is motorized.

- Batteries should be mounted securely to the device, and if possible, encased in their own compartment. An added tether may be used to secure the battery.

- The power source to a battery powered mobility device should be turned off when loading, unloading, maneuvering, or transporting the chair.

The next step is to secure the WMD using your bus's securement system. To attach the front securement straps:

- Install the track fitting end of the securement strap into a slot of the floor track or plate that is 3 to 8 inches outside the front wheel of the mobility aid. (This leaves the passenger's foot rests free and increases side-to-side stability.)

- Pull on the strap to make sure it is securely placed and locked into the track.

- Attach the other end of the strap around a solid, structural frame member of the WMD as close to the corner of the seat cushion as possible.

- Remember to maintain approximately a 45 degree angle from the floor track or plate to where the strap attaches to the WMD frame.

- Pull the loose end of the strap through the buckle until it is tight.

- Repeat this procedure with the other front strap.

To attach the rear securement straps:

- Install the track fitting end of the securement strap to the floor track or plate that is just to the inside of the mobility aid rear wheel.

- Pull on the strap to ensure that the track fitting is firmly engaged and locked into the track or plate slot.

- Attach the other end of the strap to the structural frame member of the mobility aid (as close to the corner junction of the seat cushion and seat back as possible).

- Keep a 45 degree angle on the strap between the floor track or plate to where it attaches to the WMD frame.

- Pull the loose end of the strap through the buckle until it is tight.

- Repeat this procedure with the other strap.

Check to see that all securement straps are properly tensioned and attached and that the WMD does not have any movement front-to-rear or side-to-side.

Following are some precautions to follow when securing a WMD:

- Do not attach the straps to the wheels or any detachable portion of the mobility aid.

- Do not allow the straps to conform or bend around any object (i.e. the wheels, foot rests). The securement straps must have a clear, straight load path from the floor tracks or plates to where they attach to the WMD frame.

- Keep the straps away from any sharp edges or corners.

- Never use only the cam buckle straps on all four points of attachment to the WMD frame. The cam buckle strap is primarily a slack-removing device and can only tension to the extent of the operator's strength and angle of pull. At least two of the securement strap assemblies need to have full tensioning capability (i.e., ratchet buckle or overcenter buckle).

- Do not use differing styles of buckle straps for attachment to the same end (front or rear) of the WMD. Use two of the same, identical style of buckle straps for attachment to the front, and two of the identical style of buckle straps to the rear.

- Do not cross-connect the securement strap assemblies. This will place added stress or unequal load forces on the WMD frame and may lead to collapsing or tipping of the WMD.

Securing the student

When riding in a WMD in a school bus, the student should be wearing a seatbelt that is attached to either the vehicle floor or the rear tie-down straps. Wheelchair seatbelts and positioning straps are not adequate to protect a student during a crash, or even during a sudden stop. Like the WMD securement device, you should become familiar with the manufacturer's instructions for using the shoulder/lap belts in your bus. However, here are some general guidelines for securing students riding in WMDs.

Attach the lap belt by performing the following steps:

- Place the ends of the lap belt around the student. Thread the ends through the opening between the WMD side panel and seat cushion, or through the gap between the seat back and seat cushion.

- There are two types of lap belt assemblies: parallel and integrated. Parallel lap belts will attach to the track or plate in the floor similarly to the front and rear WMD straps. Integrated lap belts will attach to the rear straps already anchored into the track or plate and attached to the rear of the WMD frame.

- Adjust the lap belt firmly and comfortably, ensuring that the buckle is placed low on the student's pelvis (near the hip) opposite the side where the shoulder belt attaches.

Attach the shoulder belt by following these steps:

- Bring the shoulder belt over the shoulder (across the collar bone) and across the upper chest of the student.

- Connect the shoulder belt to the lap belt attachment. Pull on the loose end of the belt, through the adjuster, to achieve firm but comfortable tension.

- Pull on the belt to ensure that all fittings are properly attached.

Following are some precautions regarding the lap and shoulder belts:

- The lap belt must be worn low and snug across the front of the student's pelvic bone and with the junction between the lap belt and shoulder belt located near the wearer's hip.

- Never position the lap belt over the abdominal area, over the mobility aid arm rests, or with the belt assembly twisted.

- Never extend the shoulder belt across the student's neck or face.

- Do not use postural support belts (belts that simply go around the occupant and WMD or are attached directly to the WMD) instead of an approved FMVSS certified lap belt that is designed and tested to be used in conjunction with the securement system.

Care and maintenance of WMD securement systems

It's important that the securement systems you use remain in good working order. Make sure that you inspect the straps and belts before each use, looking for cuts, frayed edges, damaged webbing, or any broken buckles or parts. Make sure items are replaced as needed.

Between uses, store the straps and belts in a clean, dry container. Storing straps and belts when not in use prevents dirt, mud, sand, and water from interfering with their function and reducing their service life. Straps and webbing will need to be periodically cleaned and any moving, mechanical, or metal-to-metal joints will need to be lubricated periodically, or as directed by the manufacturer. The floor tracks and plates should also be kept free of debris and as dry as possible.

Operating a Vehicle Lift

If your vehicle is equipped with a lift, you should be trained how to operate it and become familiar with the manufacturer's instructions. Following are some general safety precautions:

- Make sure you know how to operate the lift with power and without power.

- Inspect the lift prior to each use. Check the general appearance, all fasteners, and the lubrication of the lift. Run the lift through one cycle of operation. If you observe unusual noises or movements, contact your supervisor and do not use the lift.

- Only operate the lift with the vehicle parked on level ground. Make sure there are no objects or obstacles present that may interfere with the operation of the lift.

- Put the vehicle's emergency brake on before using the lift.

- Make sure the rollstop is working so that it raises automatically whenever the lift is off the ground.

- Read and comply with all warning labels and symbols attached to the lift.

- Never allow other students or untrained staff to operate the wheelchair lift — you are responsible for the safe use of this equipment.

Loading and unloading WMDs using a lift

The following guidelines describe how to load and unload students in WMDs using a lift.

- Know each of your passengers, their capabilities, and what they can do for themselves in the loading/unloading process. Also know how their WMDs operate: the brakes, the steering mechanism, and how to turn it on and off.

- Either have all other students off the bus or ask them to sit in their seats and remain orderly before you leave the bus to load or unload a student who uses a WMD.

- Position the vehicle so that the lift platform is level and on solid ground when in the lowered position.

- Secure the bus and remove your keys before exiting to assist a student.

- Clear a path around the vehicle before opening and securing the lift doors. Keep students, attendants and any others well away as you release and lower the lift. Make sure that the wheel locks of the student's WMD are on while the student waits for you to load him/her.

- Make sure students in WMDs are wearing wheelchair seatbelts — this is a safety requirement.

- Back the student slowly onto the lift platform. The student should be facing outward and be fully within the boundaries of the lift.

- Apply the brakes and turn off the power on power devices. (Don't rely on the lift's rollstop to keep a student from moving. The rollstop is designed to prevent slow, inadvertent rolling off the platform. The small front wheels of a quick moving WMD could hit the rollstop and tip the WMD forward, injuring the student. Also, many WMDs have larger rear wheels that could roll over the rollstop.)

- Keep a firm hold on a solid part of the WMD's frame all the time that it is on the lift.

- Ask the student (or assist the student) to put arms and feet within the confines of the device while the lift raises or lowers and when you go through the vehicle doorway.

- Let the student know when you are about to start the lift. Operate the lift smoothly, avoiding jerky movements up or down.

- Do not ride the lift with the student. (The combined weight may exceed the lift's capacity.)

- If unloading, be very careful exiting the lift. The ground is sometimes soft and the chair can tip forward as the front wheels leave the lift.

— Notes —

Special Needs Passengers

Driver _____

Instructor _____

Date _____

Location _____

Special Needs Passengers Review

1. Special needs students include children with:
   a. Physical disabilities
   b. Mental disabilities
   c. Serious medical conditions
   d. All of the above

2. When transporting special needs passengers, you should do everything for them and not let them do anything on their own.
   a. True
   b. False

3. As the driver of special needs students, your observations of student behavior can be valuable to parents and teachers.
   a. True
   b. False

4. When a special needs student begins riding the bus, it's a good idea for all parties to meet and discuss:
   a. The unique needs of the child
   b. School district policies and procedures
   c. Special circumstances of the route or vehicle equipment
   d. All of the above

5. What is **not** something you need to know about a passenger's wheeled mobility device (WMD)?
   a. Where the brakes are and how to engage and disengage them.
   b. The age of the device.
   c. How to turn a powered WMD on and off.
   d. How to steer or maneuver the WMD up and down curbs, ramps, on and off the lift, and inside the vehicle.

6. Students in WMDs should face the front of the bus.
   a. True
   b. False

7. A postural support belt is adequate for securing a student riding a bus in a WMD.
   a. True
   b. False

8. The straps securing a WMD should be attached to:
   a. The wheels
   b. The arm rests
   c. A solid part of the frame
   d. The foot rests

9. Vehicle lifts should only be operated:
   a. On level ground
   b. On an incline
   c. When the terrain is muddy
   d. In emergencies

10. When loading a student using a WMD, the WMD should be backed onto the lift platform with the student facing out.
    a. True
    b. False

Driving Techniques

Because of the nature of your role (transporting school-age children to and from their homes and school), safety must always be your top priority — especially when you're actually driving and maneuvering your vehicle.

Safely driving a vehicle as large as a school bus requires a high degree of attention, skill, and practice. This section of the handbook will discuss specific driving and maneuvering situations that you may be involved in on a daily basis. These include:

- Railroad crossings

- Intersections

- Turning

- Backing

- Driving in suburban, urban, and rural areas

Railroad Crossings

Driving across railroad crossings, or in areas where there are rail vehicles of some sort, demands special care. Careful observance of the traffic situation is your best defense.

As you approach the crossing, turn on your yellow school bus hazard warning lights and tap your brakes to warn other drivers that you are about to stop. Whether or not you are carrying any passengers, bring the bus to a complete stop between 15 to 50 feet from the rails nearest the front of the bus. On multiple-lane roads, stop in the right lane unless you have to make a left turn immediately after crossing the tracks.

Once stopped:

- Open your driver's side window and your service door so that you have an unobstructed view down both sides of the tracks.

- Turn off any noisy equipment such as radios and fans and instruct your students to be quiet.

- If your bus has manual transmission, put it into a gear that will not require shifting while you cross the tracks. (You never want to do anything that might stall your engine while crossing railroad tracks.)

- If your view of the tracks isn't adequate, don't try to cross them until you can clearly see that no train is approaching.

- If a train does pass, make sure that another train isn't coming from the other direction before you proceed.

Needless to say, if the crossing has any warning devices, or has a police officer or flagger instructing drivers, obey them. Even if there is a warning device, you should still do your own visual check before proceeding. Remember to look to see if there is enough room for your entire bus on the other side of the tracks should you have to stop immediately after crossing.

When you're certain the tracks are clear, you can move across. After safely crossing the tracks, remember to close your service door and turn off your yellow hazard warning lights.

Railroad "nevers." Following is a list of railroad "nevers." When crossing railroad tracks, never:

- Stop while on railroad tracks.

- Stop within 15 feet of railroad tracks.

- Attempt to back up once your crossing has begun.

- Attempt to pass another vehicle while crossing railroad tracks.

- Cross any railroad tracks unless there is adequate room for the entire bus to clear and fit safely on the other side.

Close calls. A close call with a train is no minor matter, so you should be prepared in advance. If the crossing gate comes down after you've started your cross, keep moving forward — even if it means breaking the gate. Should your bus stall while you're crossing, evacuate the students immediately and move them a safe distance away from the bus as quickly as possible. If your bus is stalled and a train is approaching, have everyone walk in the direction of the train at a 45 degree angle away from the tracks — this direction will put you as much out of harm's way as possible.

Finally, if you encounter any malfunctioning railroad signals or hazardous crossing conditions, report them immediately to your supervisor.

Intersections

As a professional school bus driver, negotiating intersections is one of the most common driving situations you will encounter.

If you drive in rural or suburban areas, you will encounter a lot of two-way stops and uncontrolled intersections. Even when you do not have a stop sign, always slow down and watch for other vehicles, pedestrians, and people on mopeds, bicycles, etc. Expect other traffic and always assume you do not have the right of way.

At stop signs and traffic lights, stop twice. First stop at the sign or light and then ease forward to where you can clearly see oncoming traffic. Then stop a second time.

When crossing an intersection, remember that your vehicle is larger and probably slower than a passenger car. If there is approaching cross traffic, you will need more time and space to make it safely through the intersection. Don't take chances: only cross if you are positive you have enough time. When approaching traffic lights, begin watching the light as soon as possible. If the light has been green a long time, assume it will turn yellow (and then red) by the time you get to the intersection.

A larger vehicle (such as a school bus) takes longer to stop, so be prepared. If the light turns yellow before you get to the intersection, always try to stop. Contrary to popular belief, yellow **does not** mean accelerate.

Turning

Obviously, you will need to make left- and right-hand turns while driving your bus every day. However, every turn you make is just another opportunity for you to hit something or someone, or for something or someone to hit you.

One of the best ways to safely negotiate your turns is to make sure other motorists, pedestrians, bicyclists, etc., know your intentions. Always use your turn signals and if other motorists aren't paying attention, tap your horn or flash your lights. Do whatever it takes to alert others of your presence and your intentions.

Turning safely requires that you:

- Properly set up the motor vehicle (especially for right-hand turns);

- Are alert to changing conditions;

- Anticipate the actions of others (vehicles and pedestrians); and

- Negotiate the turn slowly.

In addition, beware of the dangers of off-tracking when performing a turning maneuver. Off-tracking is a phenomenon that occurs every time a vehicle makes a turn. It means that the rear wheels of the vehicle track inside the front wheels. The longer the vehicle, the greater the off-tracking. The danger is that, in making a turn, your rear tires could ride up on the curb and hit something, including a pedestrian!

To compensate for off-tracking you need to use your **pivot point** in making a turn. Your pivot point is a conceptual point at the center of your rear axle which moves the least while your bus turns.

Right-hand turns

When making a right turn, you should pull straight out into the intersection until the curb of the street you're turning onto is even with your pivot point. Then turn your wheel hard to the right.

Now your right rear tires will easily clear the curb. It's recommended that you swing slightly to the left before making a right turn to give yourself more room.

But be careful. Don't allow more than 4 feet between your bus and the curb on your right. Vehicles behind you may think you're going straight, or taking a left turn, and try to squeeze in along your right side. Depending how close they are to your bus, you may not be able to see them there. When your bus makes its right turn, the vehicle to your right can get pinned by the off-tracking rear wheel. This is a very common cause of bus accidents.

In review, these are the steps you should follow when making a right turn:

• Signal your intentions well in advance;

• Move into the far right-hand lane (keeping at least 4 feet of space between you and the curb or parked vehicles);

• Check your mirrors for other vehicles and pedestrians;

• Reduce your speed as you approach your turn and cover your brake;

• As you begin your turn, check your mirrors again for off-tracking. Check this again half way through your turn; and

• Check your right side mirrors and complete your turn.

Left-hand turns

Left turns are usually easier than right turns. The basic procedures for making safe right turns apply to left turns too. Specifically:

- Signal your intentions well in advance;

- Check your mirrors frequently, before and during your turn;

- Move into the proper lane and make sure the intersection is clear before proceeding;

- Know the position of the other vehicles and any pedestrians around you;

- Check for fixed objects or obstacles;

- Reduce your speed as you approach your turn and cover your brake;

- As you begin your turn, check your mirrors again for off-tracking, and check this again half way through your turn; and

- Safely complete your turn.

Backing

Of all the driving maneuvers, perhaps the most difficult and dangerous is backing. This is because, when backing, you cannot see everything behind your vehicle.

With a school bus, this is even more dangerous because you are often in the vicinity of children — children who may, unthinkingly, walk into the blind area behind your vehicle or into your backing path. Because of these dangers, never back unless you absolutely have to.

When backing is unavoidable, make sure you perform the maneuver with the utmost care and caution.

Backing safely requires that you:

- Properly set up your vehicle for the maneuver;

- Thoroughly understand your immediate situation (survey your path);

- Shut off your radio, open your windows, and quiet your passengers so you can hear what is happening outside your vehicle;

- Turn on your four-way flashers to communicate to others that you're backing up. Use the back-up alarm if your vehicle has one. If your vehicle doesn't have an alarm, periodically sound your horn;

- Constantly use your mirrors;

- Go slow, and execute each backing maneuver will extreme care;

- Get out of your vehicle and visually inspect your backing situation whenever you're in doubt; and

- Never rely totally on a spotter. Remember, ultimately you are responsible for performing each backing maneuver safely.

Driving in Suburban, Urban, and Rural Areas

Suburban, urban, and rural areas have unique characteristics that you should be aware of as a school bus driver. This next section addresses issues you should keep in mind when operating in each of these areas.

Suburban driving

Driving in suburban areas presents several challenges for the professional school bus driver. As you travel on your route — going from stop to stop to your final destination — you will likely spend the majority of your time in suburban areas. As you drive in suburban areas, stay particularly alert for:

- **Pedestrians** — Many people walk, bike, skate, and use scooters in suburban areas, especially in the early morning and late afternoon — the same times you're driving your vehicle. Be aware that someone could be walking, jogging, biking, skating, or scooting in front of your bus at any time. Also keep in mind that "pedestrians on wheels" may have trouble stopping.

- **Children** — Always be alert for children who may wander or run into the street or cross in front of you. They are not as cautious as adults.

- **Uncontrolled intersections** — Uncontrolled intersections are more common in suburban areas. At every intersection, be alert for traffic coming from the other direction — and expect them not to expect you.

- **Driveways** — Scan driveways ahead to spot motorists who may pull out in front of you. Be prepared for drivers who suddenly slow down and turn into driveways without signaling.

- **Animals** — Watch for unleashed pets and the various forms of wildlife that inhabit these areas between the city and the country.

It's critical to stay alert in suburban areas and to always expect the unexpected. If you drive the same route or area every day, remain vigilant against overconfidence. The route or area may be the same, but the potential hazards — the people, vehicles, and conditions — are constantly changing.

Suburban areas also present other situations, like school zones, crossing guards, and residential areas, that require your attention.

School zone driving. As a school bus driver, you will obviously frequently be driving in school zones. Obey all speed limit and warning sign instructions. Generally, the speed limit is established at either 10 or 15 miles per hour.

Stay alert for children darting in and out of the driveway or school pick-up area. Pay particular attention to any individual(s) acting in an exiting/boarding supervisory role. These people may have a better, big picture view of the immediate situation, and will be in a good position to warn you of a possible "at risk" or unsafe situation. Follow their signals.

Crossing guards. In addition, follow all crossing guard instructions. Be alert for either hand signals or a loud whistle as the crossing guard begins to attract the attention of you and other motorists. Follow his/her instructions and watch for nearby children. Come to a complete stop when ordered to do so and do not proceed until the crossing guard gives the all-clear indication and waves you on.

Residential areas. Obey the regularly posted 25 miles per hour speed limit signs found in most residential areas. Keep in mind, many schools are located in or near residential areas.

Urban driving

Driving in an urban (or city) environment presents you with challenges you won't normally encounter in the country or suburbs. Some of these challenges include narrower and more congested streets, more incidents of "road rage" and aggressive drivers, confusing traffic signs, one-way streets, etc. The following tips and suggestions are provided to help you safely negotiate through any city-driving situation.

Whether your regular route requires you to drive in the city, or you only take an occasional field trip there, have a thorough trip plan before driving into any urban environment. Doing so will greatly enhance your chances of getting in and out of the city safely. A good trip plan should include knowing where you're going, how you're going to get there, and when.

Other city-driving tips include:

• Communicate with other drivers. Let other motorists know you're there and signal your intentions.

• Give yourself plenty of room. Reaction time and following distance is reduced in city traffic, so you must control the things you can.

• Be alert and ready for anything. This includes double parked vehicles, pedestrians, construction, detours, ambulances, etc.

- Know how to respond effectively to emergencies. Act rationally but quickly and follow proper emergency procedures.

Rural driving

Driving in the country can also present some unique challenges. Your stops will tend to be farther apart and roads will be darker in the early morning and late afternoon.

Follow these rural driving tips:

- Drive in the middle of your lane. Country roads tend to have steep and often soft shoulders. Driving on these shoulders could result in a serious rollover-type accident.

- Be especially cautious at intersections as many country intersections have one-way stops.

- Be aware of the increased danger of animals in the roadway.

Driver _____

Instructor _____

Date _____

Location _____

Driving Techniques Review

1. What is something you should **not** do when stopped before railroad tracks?
   a. Open your service door
   b. Turn off noisy equipment
   c. Back up
   d. Obey the warning devices

2. You should never cross railroad tracks unless there is enough room for your bus on the other side.
   a. True
   b. False

3. If your bus stalls on the tracks, you should evacuate the students.
   a. True
   b. False

4. If you do not have a stop sign or signal at an intersection, you can safely assume that cross traffic will stop for you.
   a. True
   b. False

5. When crossing an intersection, you should
   a. Speedily dart across traffic
   b. Step on it when you see a yellow light
   c. Realize you need more time and space than a car to make it safely through an intersection
   d. Close your eyes

6. To turn safely you must
   a. Properly set up the motor vehicle
   b. Be alert to changing conditions
   c. Negotiate the turn slowly
   d. All of the above

7. What is **not** something you should do when backing your bus?
   a. Evacuate your passengers
   b. Survey your path
   c. Turn on your four-way flashers
   d. Go slowly

8. If you're using a spotter to help you back, he/she will be responsible in case your bus hits something.
   a. True
   b. False

9. While driving in a suburban environment, you need to pay particular attention to:
   a. Pedestrians
   b. Uncontrolled intersections
   c. Driveways
   d. All of the above

10. Driving safely in city conditions requires you to:
    a. Be rude and obnoxious
    b. Be overly aggressive when looking for a parking space
    c. Use extra care and caution at all times
    d. Drink Maalox by the gallon

Defensive Driving and Emergency Maneuvers

Driving a school bus to and from school is not very hard. Driving a school bus *well* — doing everything in your power to avoid accidents, reacting effectively in emergencies, and constantly protecting the well-being of your students — is very challenging. This is the task you've chosen to undertake.

Because of the nature of your very special cargo, you need to drive better than the other motorists on the road. Since these other motorists are often distracted, rushed, aggressive, or just plain careless, you need to be even more alert and cautious. This is called *defensive driving* and it's one of the main topics in this chapter.

The other main chapter topic is emergency maneuvers. While the purpose of defensive driving is to avoid emergency situations, sometimes that will just be impossible. When you have an emergency, a school bus driver must know how to react quickly and effectively to avoid an accident. Being a professional school bus driver means a lot more than simply transporting students to and from school. It means you are responsible for their safety and well-being while they are on and around your bus. You need to do everything you can to guarantee their safety.

Defensive Driving Skills

Do you ever complain about other people's driving? Everybody does. But you're a professional school bus driver. You can make up for some of the shortcomings of others by being a better driver yourself. To do so, you need to develop the skills of a defensive driver.

A defensive driver has:

- **Excellent driving skills.** In order to be a safe and effective defensive driver, you must possess a set of good basic driving skills such as patience, common sense, and driving courtesy.

- **Good vision.** Just because you're able to pass a vision test does not mean you have good vision with regard to defensive driving. In other words, having the ability to see well is one thing. Being able to correctly process and react to what you're seeing is quite another. Good vision means you can do both.

- **Alertness.** This skill is fairly self-explanatory. As a school bus driver, you must be alert to your constantly changing driving situation. Don't let your mind get lazy due to the routine of your route. Stay sharp and expect the unexpected.

- **Sound judgement.** Giving the right-of-way to aggressive drivers, getting out of the bus to visually inspect a backing situation, and not accelerating to make it through a yellow light are all examples of sound judgement.

- **Quick reactions.** Having quick reactions means seeing the hazard, choosing the correct evasive action, and then reacting in time to avoid an accident.

Principles of Defensive Driving

The underlying principle of defensive driving is anticipating hazards *before* they occur and acting to avoid them. Driving defensively has several elements:

- Staying alert to changes by looking well ahead.

- Observing the situation.

- Recognizing potential hazards.

- Deciding on an appropriate response.

- Carrying out your plan.

Staying alert and looking ahead. One key element of defensive driving is staying alert and looking well ahead. Many drivers do not look far enough ahead to observe potential hazards in time to avoid them. Here are some guidelines:

- Scan the area ahead of you for one average block on city streets and at least a quarter of a mile on highways.

- Periodically scan to the sides while on open road.

- Always look both ways at intersections, crosswalks, construction sites, school zones, parking lots, and other areas where people may appear with little or no warning.

- Check your mirrors every four seconds and before changing your speed or position in traffic.

Observing the situation. While looking is important, you need to go to the next level of observing the overall situation. Know where you are in relation to other vehicles. Identify escape routes — empty adjacent lanes, a shoulder or median — you can use if an emergency presents itself.

Recognizing potential hazards. As you observe the overall traffic situation, you should recognize potential hazards — situations that could require you to take evasive maneuvers to avoid a collision. Potential hazards could be an inattentive driver weaving between lanes, a construction zone, an aggressive driver passing vehicles unsafely, a sharp turn ahead, or a child on a bicycle.

Deciding on an appropriate response. Once you recognize a potential hazard, you need to decide on a response. Some responses will be executed immediately, such as increasing your following distance behind an erratic driver. Others you will execute only if the situation develops into a full-blown hazard: if the driver you are following slams on his brakes, you should be prepared to stop or to take an evasive maneuver by steering into another lane.

Carrying out your plan. Once you decide on a plan, carry out any responses that can immediately make your situation safer, such as slowing down or increasing following distance. Be prepared to act on the rest of your plan if the need occurs.

Factors Impacting Defensive Driving

To be a defensive driver, you have to be ever vigilant. Sometimes, certain factors will make that more difficult, and you need to be aware of these. Factors impacting your ability to drive defensively include:

- **Light level or time of day.** Because of daylight savings as well as other factors, school bus drivers often drive during both sunrise and sunset. Be aware that these are dangerous driving times since visibility will be negatively affected by the diminished light level, and extra caution should be used.

- **Weather.** The weather can also impact your ability to drive safely and defensively. Weather also affects the road or pavement condition (for more, see the Extreme Weather chapter).

- **Driver condition.** Of all the factors that can impact your ability to drive safely, none can have a greater impact or is more important than you! As a school bus driver you must be both mentally and physically prepared to drive safely and defensively.

Emergency Maneuvers

While the goal of defensive driving is to avoid an emergency situation before it occurs, you need to be prepared to take evasive maneuvers if a hazard develops. Evasive maneuvers include evasive steering, emergency braking, and skid control. While you will probably have few or no opportunities to practice these maneuvers in advance, you should be familiar with the principles and techniques of each in case you need them in an emergency.

Evasive steering

When an emergency situation presents itself, your best option is to try to find an escape route. Many drivers don't realize it, but it's usually easier, given the size and weight of your vehicle, to steer around a hazard than to stop before a collision. The most important step in evasive steering is identifying an escape route. Depending on the circumstances, this could be another lane, the shoulder, the median, etc. Once you identify an escape route, begin your evasive steering maneuver. Use the following technique:

- Don't slam on the brakes, but, if distance permits, brake before you steer to reduce your speed. Don't brake during the evasive maneuver because it could cause you to lose control.

- Swerve only as much as necessary to clear the hazard. Turning too sharply could cause a skid or rollover.

- Turn as quickly as possible, using hand-over-hand steering. Each turn of the wheel should be about 180 degrees.

- Be prepared to counter-steer as soon as you've passed the hazard.

Emergency braking

In some situations, evasive steering may not be an option, and you will have to use emergency braking. Remember, you will be more likely to avoid a collision using emergency braking if you have maintained a safe following distance behind other vehicles. The challenge with emergency braking is to avoid over-braking. Over-braking may cause you to lose control and go into a skid. When emergency braking with traditional brakes, you may choose to use a controlled braking or stab braking technique.

- **Controlled braking.** In controlled braking, you maintain steady pressure on the brakes, applying them just short of lock-up. When control braking, keep your steering wheel movements very small. If you must make a larger steering adjustment, or if the wheels lock, release the brakes and reapply them as soon as you are in control again. Controlled braking is the best technique only if you are very knowledgeable of your vehicle. You must know how hard you can brake before losing control. If you are less familiar with the vehicle, stab braking is the better option.

- **Stab braking.** In stab braking, you fully apply the brakes until the wheels lock. Once the wheels lock, release the brakes partially, until the wheels begin to roll again. Then reapply the brakes. Continue this sequence until the vehicle has come to a safe stop.

Anti-lock braking systems. If you drive a vehicles with an anti-lock braking system (ABS), you will use a technique specific for ABS. On a vehicle with ABS, apply firm and continuous pressure on the brake pedal until you no longer need to brake. The ABS will automatically "pump" the brakes. Don't pump the brakes yourself — this will only turn the ABS on and off and make it ineffective. ABS will reduce the chances of wheel lock-up and give you greater control during braking, but only if you use it properly.

Skid control

Skids happen when the tires lose their grip on the road. This can happen because of over-accelerating, over-braking, or over-steering. Skids can affect your front wheels, rear wheels, or all your wheels at once. Skids caused by acceleration usually happen in snow, ice, or rain. Stop skids by taking your foot off the accelerator. If you have a manual transmission, push in the clutch: this disengages the wheels from the power of the engine, allowing them to roll freely again and, hopefully, to regain traction. Rear-wheel braking skids happen when the rear drive wheels lock. Since sliding wheels move faster than wheels with traction, the vehicle will begin to slide sideways and go into a spin as the rear end tries to "overtake" the front end of the vehicle. To correct this type of skid:

- **Stop braking.** This will let the rear wheels roll again and keep them from sliding any further. If you're on ice and have a manual transmission, push in the clutch to let the wheels turn freely.

- **Turn quickly.** When your vehicle begins to slide sideways, quickly steer in the direction you want to go.

- **Counter-steer if needed.** As the vehicle turns back on course, it has a tendency to keep right on turning. Unless you turn your steering wheel quickly the other way, you may find yourself sliding in the opposite direction.

— Notes —

Defensive Driving and Emergency Maneuvers

Driver _____

Instructor _____

Date _____

Location _____

Defensive Driving and Emergency Maneuvers Review

1. What is **not** a skill of the defensive driver?
    a. Good vision
    b. Alertness
    c. Sound judgement
    d. A hearty appetite

2. The underlying principle of defensive driving is anticipating hazards *before* they occur and acting to avoid them.
    a. True
    b. False

3. Which is **not** a core skill for avoiding accidents and emergency situations:
    a. Recognizing the hazard
    b. Understanding the correct evasive maneuver
    c. Acting in time
    d. Taking side streets whenever possible

4. Many drivers fail to look far enough ahead.
    a. True
    b. False

5. Once you recognize a potential road hazard, you should:
    a. Get off the road immediately
    b. Accelerate and swerve around the hazard
    c. Decide on an appropriate response
    d. Call your supervisor for advice

6. What elements can negatively affect your ability to drive defensively?
   a. Time of day and light level
   b. The weather
   c. Your mental and physical condition
   d. All of the above

7. Emergency maneuvers are not a big concern because you practice them every day.
   a. True
   b. False

8. When you encounter a road hazard, your best course of action is always to brake as hard as possible.
   a. True
   b. False

9. Controlled braking and stab braking are two forms of emergency braking.
   a. True
   b. False

10. To correct a skid, you should:
    a. Stop braking
    b. Steer in the direction you want the bus to go
    c. Counter-steer if necessary
    d. All of the above

Speed and Space Management

Two common ingredients in most large vehicle accidents are speeding and tailgating. Speeding is defined as driving over the posted limit or driving too fast for the current conditions. Tailgating is defined as following another vehicle too closely to avoid an accident. Both speeding and tailgating are driver errors that can be eliminated by proper driving habits including proper speed and space management.

You already know speeding in the most ideal conditions is unsafe. But when you combine speeding with poor space management, you're creating an extremely dangerous and high-risk situation.

Good speed management means adjusting your vehicle's speed to current traffic, weather, and road conditions. Good space management means allowing an adequate and safe space between you and the vehicle(s) directly in front, behind, and to the sides of your bus.

This chapter of your handbook discusses ways you can prevent accidents by managing your speed (slowing down) and your space (developing a safety cushion) between your bus and other vehicles.

Speed Management

We're all affected by the pressures of time. In today's hectic, fast-paced and often stress-filled environment, we often feel rushed — especially when we're in our vehicles.

When you're driving against the clock, it's a normal reaction to step on the accelerator and start and stop quickly in order to try and stay on schedule. Almost all of us have demonstrated this type of driving behavior. But how much time are we really saving when we speed — five minutes, three, 30 seconds? The fact is, we're really not gaining that much time, certainly not enough to justify putting ourselves and others at risk.

Bottom line: The best reasons not to speed are to avoid dangerous situations and to prevent accidents. Speed is dangerous, and can be deadly. The professional school bus driver should obey all posted speed limits and drive with due regard to existing traffic conditions. Some driving conditions (such as road construction or severe weather) dictate that you drive at lower speeds. At other times you may have to keep up with the current flow of traffic (such as on an expressway) in order not to become a hazard for others.

Keep in mind when you're driving your bus that the faster you go, the longer it will take to stop. Large vehicles like school buses take longer to stop than passenger vehicles traveling at the same speed. The average passenger vehicle traveling at 50 mph can stop in about 190 feet. However, a large vehicle traveling at the same speed can take over 300 feet to stop.

There are three factors that need to be considered when determining your stopping distance. In order, they are:

1. **Perception distance.** Perception distance is the distance your bus travels from the time you perceive a hazard in front of you until your brain registers it as dangerous. On average, this process (seeing, then recognizing the hazard) takes about three-quarters of a second. At 55 mph, the perception distance would be 60 feet.

2. **Reaction distance.** Reaction distance is the distance your bus travels from the time your brain registers the hazard until it sends the message to your leg and foot to to apply the brakes. Most drivers need an additional three-quarters of a second for this, or another 60 feet at 55 mph.

3. **Braking distance.** Braking distance is the actual distance your bus needs to come to a complete stop after you apply the brakes. Many factors can affect braking distance including the speed, weight and size of your vehicle, the condition of your brakes, and current road conditions. While your perception and reaction distances will be the same in any vehicle you drive, braking distance is considerably longer in a large vehicle. For instance, a fully-loaded semi truck will take 4.8 seconds (or 390 feet) to come to a complete stop when traveling 55 mph. While your vehicle is not quite that large or heavy, you must account for your increased braking distance when in your school bus.

Pavement condition and speed management

Wet or icy pavement conditions can dramatically increase your stopping distance. A curve you can normally take at 45 mph on dry pavement could result in a serious skid or even rollover on wet or icy pavement at the same speed. In these conditions, it's important to slow down a recommended five miles below the posted limit — even more if you feel it necessary to maintain the safety of yourself and your passengers.

Driving at night and speed management

Maintaining good speed management habits is especially important when driving at night. You should increase your following distance and reduce your speed when driving at night. In addition, you should never out-drive your headlights.

Out-driving your headlights means you cannot safely stop your bus before you pass an object illuminated by your lights ahead of you on or near the roadway. If this is the case, you need to slow down.

To review, safely managing speed requires:

- Obeying posted speed limits;

- Driving with due regard given to existing traffic;

- Adjusting speed with regard to weather and other road conditions; and

- Not out-driving your vehicle's headlights (night driving).

Space Management

Maintaining good vehicle space management is essential to safe driving. Good space management means you should maintain a safety cushion of space between you and the vehicle(s) in front, behind, and to the sides of you. In addition, you also need to be aware of the space above and below your bus. There are three keys to doing this, including:

1. **Using your eyes.** Visual scanning should become a habit for whatever and whenever you're driving. You need to develop a routine of checking all four sides of the vehicle.

2. **Using your mirrors.** Your bus should be equipped with mirrors that allow you to see virtually every aspect of the vehicle. Use of your mirrors should be second nature. Mirror scanning should be an integral part of your visual scanning routine. In addition, keep all your mirrors clean, and make sure they are properly adjusted.

3. **Using your judgement.** Your good judgement, combined with common sense, will help you control and safely manage space.

Space management to your front

Since many large vehicle accidents involve running into the vehicle in front, the safety cushion in front of you becomes extremely important. Never tailgate!

You should have at least one second of cushion for each 10 feet of vehicle length under 40 mph. Over that, add at least one second to the total. This means if your bus is about 40 feet in length, you should maintain a four second cushion of space between you and the vehicle in front of you at speeds of 40 mph or less.

Avoiding front-end collisions requires:

• Maintaining a safe following distance;

• Being alert to obstructions on the road; and

• Not out-driving your vehicle's headlights (when driving at night)

Space management to your rear

While you may have total control of your front safety cushion, cars and other vehicles tailgating you is another story. If another vehicle is riding your tail, and you are forced to stop suddenly, the following vehicle is at great risk of rear-ending your bus.

Therefore, it's important for you to help keep these unsafe drivers out of trouble by frequently checking your mirrors, staying in the far right-hand lane whenever possible, maintaining a constant speed, and avoiding sudden lane changes.

These safe driving behaviors allow unsafe and aggressive tailgaters to more easily pass you.

To review, you can avoid rear-end collisions by:

- Maintaining an adequate margin of safety behind your bus;

- Checking your mirrors frequently to watch for possible tailgaters; and

- Letting close-following vehicles pass when it is safe to do so.

Space management to your sides

Frequent use of your mirrors and windows is essential if you're to spot potentially dangerous situations or drivers to the left and right of your bus. In addition, stay in the center of your lane, and signal your intentions early when making a lane change or turn, so other motorists can anticipate your actions.

Space management above and below

You also need to be aware of the space directly above and below your vehicle. Be aware of low-hanging tree branches and signs, phone and power wires, or any other over-head object that could come in contact with your bus. Be attentive at all times to your immediate driving situation.

From below, watch for road debris and pot holes that could damage your bus or cause you to lose control.

Space management for merging

Entering and exiting traffic safely requires both your undivided attention and sound space management. You have to ensure there is sufficient room and time to merge into and out of traffic.

Whether you're pulling out of a school parking lot or accelerating up a freeway on-ramp, safely merging into traffic requires:

- Signaling your intentions well in advance;

- Planning ahead and being patient when waiting for an opening;

- Accelerating to merge (or make your turn) smoothly; and

- Constantly checking your mirrors.

Safely merging out of traffic requires:

- Signaling your intentions well in advance;

- Safely moving to the proper lane;

- Planning ahead and being patient when waiting for an opening;

- Reducing speed (or stopping) to exit (or turn) smoothly; and

- Constantly checking your mirrors.

— Notes —

Speed and Space Management

Driver _____

Instructor _____

Date _____

Location _____

Speed and Space Management Review

1. What are the two definitions of speeding used in this chapter?
    a. Driving too fast for conditions
    b. Making up for lost time
    c. Driving faster than the posted speed limit
    d. Both a and c

2. What is **not** a part of safely managing speed?
    a. Getting there first
    b. Driving consistent with posted speed limits
    c. Driving with due regard for existing traffic conditions
    d. Adjusting your speed according to current weather and road conditions

3. Perception distance is:
    a. The distance your bus travels before your brain tells your leg to step on the brake
    b. The distance your bus travels after the brakes have been applied
    c. The distance your bus travels from the time you see a hazard until the time your brain recognizes it
    d. The distance (in estimated miles) of your route

4. Reaction distance is:
    a. The distance your bus travels from when your brain reacts to a hazard to the moment your foot applies the brake
    b. The distance (in actual miles) of your route
    c. The distance your bus travels after the brakes have been applied
    d. The distance your bus travels from the time you see a hazard until the time your brain recognizes it

5. Braking distance is:
    a. The distance your bus travels before your next scheduled break
    b. The distance your bus travels before you hit the brakes
    c. The distance it takes for your bus to come to a complete stop after applying the brakes
    d. The distance between your brake pedal and the floor

6. On wet or icy road conditions, it's a good idea to drive:
   a. A minimum of 5 mph below the posted limit, and slower if necessary
   b. 10 mph below the posted limit
   c. 15 mph below the posted limit
   d. Stay at home and let the children walk to school

7. A safety cushion is:
   a. Something you sit on while driving to help prevent a sore back
   b. A designated school bus parking zone found at most schools
   c. An area of space in the front, back, and to the sides of your bus that separates your bus from other vehicles
   d. An extra absorbent front or rear bumper

8. The three keys to managing your space are:
   a. Your hand, eye, and foot coordination
   b. Your intuition, ESP ability, and innate sense of danger
   c. Your ears, nose, and throat
   d. Your eyes, mirrors, and good judgement

9. If, when checking your mirrors, you notice you're being tailgating, you should:
   a. Slam on your brakes to teach the other driver a good lesson
   b. Make a sudden lane change to get out of the driver's way
   c. Gradually slow down, or safely change lanes to allow the other motorist to pass
   d. Open your window and wave the other driver by

10. Safely merging into traffic does **not** require that you:
    a. Signal your intentions well in advance
    b. Accelerate quickly, look for an opening, then dart into traffic
    c. Build speed gradually to merge smoothly into traffic
    d. Constantly check your mirrors

Seeing Hazards

In a previous chapter, we discussed the importance of defensive driving. A key element of defensive driving — and staying safe on the road — is seeing and identifying hazards.

Obviously, most drivers are continually gazing out their windshield and windows, but many are only *looking* and not truly *seeing* what is around them. You need to go to that next level of truly *seeing* and interpreting the driving picture around you so that you can make the appropriate decisions.

In this chapter, we'll talk about these elements of seeing hazards:

- Using your mirrors

- Scanning techniques

- Avoiding dangerous situations

- Adjusting for restricted visibility

Using Your Mirrors

Because of your bus's limited visibility, you will have to rely heavily on your mirrors. Mirrors allow you to see around the bus and eliminate many of the vehicle's blind spots. They also allow you to watch your rear axle while you're turning and are essential for you to perform any backing maneuvers.

Mirror adjustment

For your mirrors to be effective, however, they must be properly adjusted. Clean your mirrors and check their adjustment at the beginning of each day's trip. If you have trouble adjusting the mirrors yourself, have another person help you.

How do you know that your mirrors are properly adjusted? Read the follow section to find out what you should see in each of your mirrors.

Left flat mirror. You should see the left side of the bus along the inside edge of your left mirror. The horizon should be about one-third to one-fourth from the top of the mirror. Your rear tires should be barely visible, touching the mirror's bottom edge. Overall, you should see about 200 feet (four bus lengths) behind your vehicle.

Right flat mirror. You should see the right side of the bus along the inside edge of your right mirror. The horizon should be about one-fourth from the top of the mirror — slightly higher than it is in your left mirror. (This adjustment gives you the best view of the front, right side, and rear of your bus.) You should be able to see about 200 feet (four bus lengths) in back of the bus.

Convex mirrors. Your convex mirrors, located below the outside flat mirrors, can help you see areas that your regular flat mirrors cannot. Their outward curvature provides a wide-angle view.

Adjust your convex mirrors so you can see the entire area along the side of the bus. Each convex mirror should also allow you to see at least one traffic lane to the side of the bus. Remember that convex mirrors make objects appear farther away than they actually are. Assume that anything in your convex mirrors is directly beside your bus.

Crossview mirrors. On buses where the engine compartment is in front of your windshield, you may have crossview mirrors mounted on your front fender. Adjust the crossview mirrors so you can see the entire area in front of the vehicle and the front bumper.

Inside mirror. The inside mirror allows you to keep an eye on your students. Adjust the mirror so you can see all of the students, including the tops of the students right behind you. You should be able to see the top of the rear window in the top of your mirror.

Seat adjustment

While it may not automatically occur to you, proper seat adjustment goes hand-in-hand with adjusting your mirrors. A properly adjusted seat will let you get the maximum visibility from your mirrors and out of your windshield.

Before moving your mirrors, first make sure your seat is in a comfortable position where you can operate the foot controls and reach the steering wheel easily. Seat height is important too: to prevent cutting off the circulation in your legs, adjust the seat so there is no pressure against the bottom of your thighs when you operate the accelerator. When your seat is adjusted properly, you can move your mirrors to get the best view around your bus.

Mirror use

The key to using your mirrors is to check them quickly and consistently and to understand what you see. You should:

- Check your mirrors every five to eight seconds and before you change lanes or your position in traffic.

- Look back and forth between your mirrors and the road in front of you. If you focus on your mirrors too long, you'll miss out on the action ahead.

- Be aware that the view in your mirrors may be different from the actual situation. Convex mirrors, for instance, make objects appear smaller and farther away.

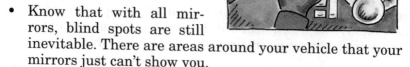

- Know that with all mirrors, blind spots are still inevitable. There are areas around your vehicle that your mirrors just can't show you.

Even with their limitations, mirrors are valuable tools that increase your ability to see. Don't jeopardize your safety, or the safety of others, by not using them or using them incorrectly.

Scanning Techniques

Seeing hazards is not as automatic as you may think. You need to take a systematic approach to scanning for hazards, and stay mindful of your scanning techniques, to increase your chances of spotting a hazard in time to react safely and effectively.

When scanning:

- Keep your eyes continually moving. Scan for hazards all around your bus — in front, to the sides, and behind your vehicle.

- Look well ahead of your bus. You want to look at least one and a half blocks ahead of your vehicle on city streets and a quarter mile ahead in the country or on the highway. This is where your bus will be in the next 15 seconds.

- Scan your mirrors every five to eight seconds to keep track of what is happening to the sides and rear of the bus.

- Maintain a proper following distance. In order to effectively take in the traffic picture and to react to potentially dangerous situations, you must leave yourself enough room. Remember, you want to leave about four seconds of distance between you and the vehicle in front of you when you are traveling at less than 40 mph; if traveling over this speed, leave at least five seconds of following distance. (See the Speed and Space Management chapter for more info on following distance.)

- Be especially alert in areas with more traffic and pedestrian activity. These areas include school zones, intersections, construction sites, hospital zones, and fire stations.

- Identify potential hazards from other road users and the road itself.

- Pay attention to traffic signs and signals. These are often clues that will help you anticipate the actions of other drivers.

- Beware of highway hypnosis. When traveling long stretches of highway, be careful that you do not fall into highway hypnosis — a state where you look out your windows, but fail to really *see* what you are looking at. Take extra care to keep your eyes moving and your mind alert in "uneventful" driving conditions.

- Avoid complacency. You may drive the same route day-in and day-out, which makes it easy to think you know all the route's dangerous areas. However, while your route stays the same, the vehicles, drivers, and other conditions are always changing. Vigilant scanning will help you spot the unexpected.

Avoiding Dangerous Situations

The purpose of scanning is to spot potentially dangerous situations before they become full-blown emergencies requiring evasive maneuvers. By spotting the situations early, you can take action to avoid a possible accident.

To avoid a dangerous situation, however, you have to recognize that the situation is dangerous. Dangerous situations can be caused by:

- User hazards, or

- Road hazards

User hazards

Other vehicles. It would be nice if all the other drivers on the road were as well-trained and as concerned about safety as you are. Unfortunately, this is not the case. Other drivers may be confused, distracted, impaired, or driving aggressively. Learn to recognize these clues from potentially dangerous drivers:

- **Confused drivers.** Drivers who are unfamiliar with an area may stop, turn, change lanes, or exit the highway with little or no warning. Out-of-state license plates or car-top luggage carriers are good clues that a driver may be in unfamiliar territory. Also be alert for drivers who are focused on street signs, maps, or building numbers. You may also see signs of hesitation, such as driving very slowly or braking often. If a driver seems confused, increase your following distances and be prepared for them to act suddenly and without warning. Be alert to street and traffic signs that may tip you off to their next actions.

- **Distracted drivers.** The phenomenon of cell phones has led to a dramatic increase in distracted driving. If you spot a driver talking into a phone, realize his/her mind is not completely on the road. However, other things can lead to distraction too. If you take note of what people are actually  doing in their vehicles, you will see drivers eating, putting on makeup, tending to children, changing clothes, pulling items out of the back seat, and even reading while they are driving down the road. You may also see distracted drivers weaving from lane to lane, erratically speeding up or slowing down, or making sudden movements (like exiting the highway) with no warning. Give these distracted drivers a wide berth.

- **Impaired drivers.** Drivers impaired by alcohol, drugs, or extreme fatigue are very dangerous on the roadway. You may encounter these drivers at any time of day, but be especially vigilant if you ever drive late at night (such as on a field trip). Drivers who are weaving from lane to lane, speeding up and slowing down, or hitting their brakes for no apparent reason, may be impaired. Dramatically increase your following distance if you suspect a driver may be impaired and, if possible, contact local authorities to report the driver.

- **Angry or aggressive drivers.** Aggressive driving has become a major concern as incidents of "road rage" have made major news headlines. Aggressive drivers may tailgate you, honk, flash their lights, swerve in front of you and hit their brakes, or gesture at your bus. Give these drivers a wide berth and resist any temptation to respond. Responding to aggressive drivers will likely only make the situation worse, and you do not know how far they will take their actions.

Other road users. Not everyone using the road, of course, is in a vehicle. You need to be aware of other road users, such as walkers, joggers, and bicyclists, and the hazards they present as well. Once you spot these other road users, stay aware of them until you safely pass them. When the walkers or bicyclists are children, be extra attentive. Children often act more impulsively and are not as cautious as adults.

Road hazards

Road hazards are the characteristics of the road's surface, shape, or contour that can affect your ability to see or control your vehicle, resulting in a potentially dangerous situation. They may appear in many different forms and can be man-made, naturally occurring, or a combination of the two. Some examples include:

- Sharp curves

- Uneven road surfaces

- Pot holes

- Drop-offs

- Construction zones

- Icy, snowy, or wet road surfaces

- Debris on the road

All of these situations would require you to slow down, heighten your alertness, and think about what actions you can take to lessen the danger of the situation. If you have been looking far enough ahead, and systematically scanning the road scene, you should be able to recognize road hazards far enough in advance to avoid a dangerous situation or the need to make emergency maneuvers.

Adjusting for Restricted Visibility

Although you may be looking ahead, scanning for hazards, and getting optimum use of your mirrors, some situations will still make it difficult for you to see hazards. Your bus itself, for instance, has several blind spots where it is difficult to see hazards. You need to be aware of these areas and how you can reduce the danger they present.

In other situations, lighting or weather will make it hard to see. The cardinal rule in these situations is to slow down and increase your following distance from other vehicles. This will give you more time to react to hazards.

The Danger Zone

We talked about the Danger Zone in the Passenger Safety chapter of this book, but it bears repeating here. You must be particularly aware of this area of restricted visibility when you operate a school bus.

The Danger Zone is an area 10 feet in front of, behind, and on each side of your bus. A student standing immediately in front of your bus will probably be invisible to you. Likewise, several cars or students could be behind your bus and completely hidden from view. And even with proper adjustment of your crossview mirrors, it will be difficult to see some areas on the sides of your bus.

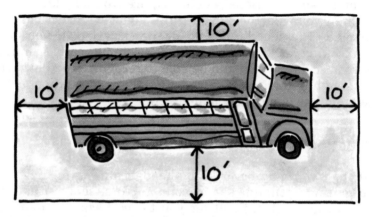

How do you compensate for the Danger Zone?

- **Teach your students.** Teach your students about the Danger Zone and the importance of staying at least 10 feet from the bus at all times. Educate them about proper loading and unloading procedures so they know how to stay out of your blind spots.

- **Enforce the rules.** Staying out of the Danger Zone is not just something you must teach your students, it's a rule you have to enforce. When students ignore the Danger Zone rules, you must talk to them and remind them that this is a critical rule for their safety — don't ever let this one slide.

- **Keep vigilant track of students getting on and off the bus.** Just because you've taught them about the Danger Zone and reinforced the rules doesn't mean your passengers will always remember or obey your directions. You must vigilantly keep track of your passengers as they board and depart your bus. If there is ever a time you cannot account for a student, get out of your bus and make sure he/she is not in the Danger Zone and hidden from view.

- **Keep track of vehicles.** It's not only students that can become hidden in the Danger Zone. While driving, vehicles may disappear from view while in the blind areas of the Danger Zone. Continually check your mirrors to see if a vehicle is entering these blind areas. Don't change lanes until the vehicle is back in sight. Adjust your own speed, if necessary, so that the vehicle doesn't remain in a blind spot.

- **Don't back.** The area behind your bus is completely hidden from view, making backing a very dangerous maneuver. Do not back your bus unless absolutely necessary. If you must back, get out of the vehicle and check your path before you begin.

Besides the Danger Zone, the structure of your vehicle may present other blind spots. Mirrors themselves can cause blind spots, as can the support beams in either corner of your windshield. Learn where these blind spots are so you can compensate when driving and loading and unloading your passengers.

Sunlight

Sunlight is generally your friend, making it easier to see and perform your driving tasks. However, there are times when sunlight can actually reduce your ability to see.

- **Extremely bright sunlight** can cause almost blinding glare as it's reflected by snow, glass, or even the road surface. Sunglasses and your bus's sun visor can help you block out some of the excessive light. Also, keep your windshield and mirrors  clean. When these items are dirty, they intensify the visibility problems caused by glare.

- **Dawn and dusk driving**, when the sun is low in the sky, can be very difficult. If you are driving into the sun, it can be almost blinding. Again, sunglasses and your visor can help. When driving away from the sun, be aware that other drivers cannot see you very well because of these conditions. If you are driving right after the sun goes down, or just before it comes up, the sky will be bright but the road will be very dark. Try using your sun visor to block off as much of the bright sky as possible. This will let your pupils enlarge, enabling you to see the dark road better.

Night driving

Darkness reduces visibility, making night driving more challenging than driving during the day. Following are some of the specific factors that make night driving more challenging and how you can compensate for them:

- **Your eyes simply don't see as well at night or in dim light.** This problem increases as people get older. *How to compensate:* One way to help your night vision is by wearing sunglasses during the day to reduce eye strain. Also, turning off inside lights and dimming your instrument panel will help you see better outside. Signal all stops and turns a little earlier than you would during daylight to give others more time to react. Increase your own following distance by at least one second.

- **Headlights do not allow you to see as far as you can in daylight.** With headlights, you'll only be able to see about 250 feet with your low beams and 350 to 500 feet with your high beams (and this is if the weather is good.) *To compensate:* To be safe, you need to adjust your speed to keep your stopping distance within your sight distance. Use your highbeams when it's safe and legal to do so to maximize visibility.

- **Headlight glare can temporarily blind drivers.** *To compensate:* Don't look directly at bright lights when driving. If an oncoming driver has bright headlights, watch the side of the road until the vehicle passes. To

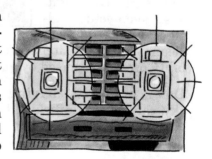

avoid blinding others, dim your own lights when you are within 500 feet of an oncoming vehicle. As in sunlight, dirt and grime on your windshield or mirrors will increase glare, so make sure these items are clean before driving at night.

- **Lighting is poor or confusing.** On most highways, there are no lights, leaving you entirely dependent on your headlights. In urban areas where there is illumination, traffic signals and hazards can be hard to see against a background of signs, shop windows, and other lights. *To compensate:* Slow down.

Fog, snow, and rain

Fog, snow, and rain can greatly reduce your visibility, as well as causing other problems in controlling your vehicle. To compensate for the lost visibility, you must slow down and increase your following distance behind other vehicles. See the Extreme Weather chapter in this handbook for a complete discussion of these driving conditions.

— Notes —

Driver _____

Instructor _____

Date _____

Location _____

Seeing Hazards Review

1. Mirrors eliminate all the blind areas around your bus.
    a. True
    b. False

2. Which is **not** something you need to do before driving your bus.
    a. Adjust your seat
    b. Adjust your mirrors
    c. Clean your mirrors
    d. Clean your tires

3. Effectively scanning the traffic scene will increase your chances of spotting a hazard in time to avoid an accident.
    a. True
    b. False

4. When scanning:
    a. Focus on the area immediately in front of your bus
    b. Identify potential hazards
    c. Focus on your mirrors and look out the windshield every five to eight seconds
    d. Ignore street and traffic signs

5. Where should you be looking when driving?
    a. One and a half blocks ahead when in the city
    b. A quarter mile ahead in the country or when on a highway
    c. Where your bus will be in the next 15 seconds
    d. All of the above

6. To avoid dangerous situations, you should try to spot user hazards and road hazards.
   a. True
   b. False

7. Which drivers are **not** a hazard on the road?
   a. Experienced drivers
   b. Angry drivers
   c. Distracted drivers
   d. Confused drivers

8. If you see a construction zone ahead, you should:
   a. Slow down
   b. Heighten your alertness
   c. Think about what actions you can take to make your situation safer
   d. All of the above

9. There is nothing you can do to compensate for reduced visibility.
   a. True
   b. False

10. What is an effective way of compensating for reduced visibility at night?
    a. Turning on all your interior lights
    b. Focusing your eyes on approaching headlights
    c. Reducing your speed and increasing your following distance
    d. Using your highbeam headlights at all times

Breakdowns and Accidents

No one wants to think about having a vehicle breakdown or accident, but these events are definite possibilities that are best prepared for in advance. One of the best ways to avoid breakdowns and accidents caused by mechanical problems is to perform a thorough pre-trip inspection before every trip. This chapter will cover pre-trip inspections, as well as how to handle breakdowns, accidents, emergency evacuations, fires, and first aid situations.

Pre-trip Inspections

While you are a driver and not a mechanic, you do have a certain level of responsibility for the mechanical condition of your vehicle. Every day, you must make sure your vehicle is in sound operating condition.

A proper pre-trip inspection serves several purposes:

- Most importantly, you may catch an unsafe condition *before* it causes an accident.

- You can spot mechanical problems before they lead to breakdowns on the road.

- By avoiding breakdowns, you will not have to contend with your bus route being thrown off schedule, upset or nervous students, or anxious parents.

- Catching mechanical problems early will help your maintenance department control costs.

- Pre-trip inspections are often required by law and/or company policy.

Pre-trip inspections are required by federal regulations governing commercial vehicles. If you are performing operations that fall under federal regulations (see the Compliance chapter), you are required to perform this inspection. Most state regulations also require school bus drivers to perform pre-trip inspections. Check with your supervisor about any specific state requirements.

But far beyond complying with any regulations, a careful and thorough pre-trip is just good safety practice. The pre-trip inspection should be part of your daily routine — do it the same way each day so it becomes a habit and you are less likely to miss something. The following seven-step routine is recommended:

- **Vehicle overview.** Walk around your bus and note its overall condition. Look for body damage or any fluids leaking from the vehicle. If a vehicle inspection report was prepared from the previous day/trip, review the report.

- **Engine compartment.** Open the vehicle hood and check all the fluid levels (oil, coolant, power steering, transmission, windshield washer); inspect hoses and belts for wear or looseness; check the alternator, water pump, and air compressor (if applicable).

- **Inside the vehicle.** Start your bus and check all of your gauges for normal readings; check the steering wheel, clutch, brakes, and windshield wipers; clean and adjust mirrors if necessary;

make sure all your safety equipment (fire extinguisher, first aid kit, emergency triangles, etc.) is present and in good condition.

- **Lights.** Turn off the engine and turn on all your lights. Go to the front of the bus and check the lights.

- **Walkaround.** Turn off the headlights but leave the rest of your lights on. Walk around your bus, starting on the driver's side. Check each wheel and axle, the steering system, the fuel tank area, suspension components, and each light and reflector.

- **Signal lights.** Get in the vehicle, turn off your warning lights, and turn on the left signal light. Get out of the bus and check to make sure the signal is working. Repeat with the right signal. Check the brake lights with a helper.

- **Brake system.** Start the engine, drive forward, and then test your brakes. If you have air brakes, you should make sure that the air pressure is building at the specified rate and that your emergency brakes activate when there is a loss of pressure.

Hopefully your vehicle will check out fine and you will be able to start your day after completing the pre-trip. If there are any problems, however, report them to your supervisor immediately. Never take an unsafe vehicle on the road.

Inspection reports

If you are involved in operations falling under federal regulations, you will be required to fill out a driver vehicle inspection report covering several specific components of your vehicle. On the report, you should list and describe any equipment problems you found during your inspections or the course of your work day. Any defect or deficiency must be corrected (or your company must certify that correction is not necessary to safely operate the vehicle) before the vehicle can be driven again.

If you do not fall under federal regulations, you may still have to fill out a written report to meet state or company/school requirements. Ask your supervisor about any inspection reports you are required to complete.

Breakdowns

Despite the best maintenance, you could have a mechanical breakdown while on the road. You will be better prepared if you think about how to handle a breakdown *before* one occurs.

In the case of a breakdown, follow these general procedures:

- Get your bus safely off the road. You do not want to be a hazard to other vehicles.

- Put out emergency warning devices to warn other drivers. (More on this shortly.)

- Contact your company/school by radio or cell phone. Advise them of your situation and location.

- If you are unable to reach your company/school, try to flag down a passing motorist that can call on your behalf.

- As a last resort, you may send a couple older, responsible students to a nearby house or business to make the phone call. **Under no circumstances should you leave your bus or passengers to make the call.** You are responsible for the safety of your students at all times — you cannot leave them unattended.

- Keep your students calm and on the bus. The bus is almost always the safest place for your passengers in the case of a breakdown. Evacuation could be necessary, however, if you were unable to get the bus off the road and were stopped in a dangerous spot, such as on railroad tracks or the middle of the highway.

Emergency warning devices

Whenever you must stop along the roadside, because of breakdown or an accident, you are responsible for warning other drivers of your presence. The best way to do this is by putting out warning devices.

If federal regulations apply to your bus, you must put out warning devices within 10 minutes if you have an accident or breakdown. Federal regulations require commercial drivers to carry three reflective triangles, three flares capable of burning for at least 1 hour, or six fusees capable of burning for at least 30 minutes. These devices must be placed in a specified way depending on the situation.

Following are the federal requirements for placing emergency warning devices. Even if federal regulations do not apply to your bus or operations, these are still good guidelines for warning device placement whenever you have a breakdown or accident.

Breakdowns/accidents on two-lane roads. Place the devices as follows:

- One 10 feet from the vehicle, facing oncoming traffic. This device can be placed at the front or rear of the vehicle, depending on traffic direction.

- One 100 feet from the vehicle, in the center of the lane or shoulder where you are stopped, facing oncoming traffic.

- One 100 feet from the vehicle in the direction opposite oncoming traffic.

Breakdowns/accidents on divided highways or one-way roads. Place the devices as follows:

- Place all devices on the traffic side of the vehicle, facing oncoming traffic.

- Place the devices at 10 feet, 100 feet, and 200 feet from the rear of the vehicle.

Breakdowns/accidents on a curve or hill. If you have a breakdown or accident within 500 feet of a curve or crest of a hill, place the devices as follows:

- Place the first two devices according to the rules for two-lane or divided highways.

- Place the third device 100 to 500 feet from the vehicle in the direction of the visual obstruction. This will give drivers time to react.

Accidents

While school buses generally have outstanding safety records, you could still be involved in an accident while driving your bus. Accidents, even minor ones, can throw the involved drivers into an emotional reaction. The important thing, however, is for you to keep your head and react appropriately to ensure the safety of your passengers and other involved motorists.

If you are involved in an accident (or come across an accident involving other drivers) there are some standard procedures you should follow at the accident scene. Familiarizing yourself with these procedures ahead of time will help you react appropriately.

- **Stop immediately.** Failure to stop when you are in an accident is a criminal offense. Stay calm and move your vehicle as far off the road as possible.

- **Prevent other accidents.** Turn on your four-way flashers as an immediate warning to other drivers. Set out emergency warning devices. (The proper position of warning devices was described in the "Breakdowns" section of this chapter.)

- **Calm your passengers.** If the accident is somewhat serious, it could be very traumatic for your young passengers. Try to quickly calm them and get them to pay attention to you. They must follow your instructions without hesitation for their safety.

- **Decide if you need to evacuate.** In most situations, your passengers are safest remaining on the school bus. However, if you are stopped in a dangerous spot (such as on railroad tracks) or if there is a fire, you will have to get your students off the bus.

- **Evacuate if necessary.** Follow the evacuation procedures discussed in the following section.

- **Help the injured.** Are any of your students or the other motorists injured? Phone or radio for medical help or get someone else to make the call. Provide first aid if you are able. Hopefully you will be trained in first aid procedures, but even if you aren't, remember that your efforts could mean the difference between life and death. (Also, most states have laws protecting "good Samaritans" from legal liability.) At minimum, keep the victims warm and do not move them unless they are in immediate danger.

- **Contact law enforcement.** Call directly, if possible, or radio or call your school/company and have them contact the police. If you are unable to contact your school/company, flag down a motorist to make the call, have a student flag down a motorist or — as a last resort — send a couple responsible, older students to a nearby home or business and instruct them to make the call. **Under no circumstances should you leave your bus.** You are still responsible for the safety of your other passengers.

- **Document the accident.** Write down the names, license numbers, and other information regarding the accident. Take photos or draw some simple diagrams while the scene is fresh in your mind.

- **Call your company/school.** If you didn't contact the police through your company/school, try to radio or call now. Report the full details of the accident to your company as soon as possible.

- **Complete a preliminary accident form.** If you carry accident forms or reporting kits, try to fill out this material now

Emergency Evacuations

Fortunately, evacuations are not necessary in most school bus emergencies. Most of the time, your passengers are safest staying on the bus. But when an evacuation is necessary, the procedures for getting your students off the bus should be followed as closely as possible.

First, calmly give your students clear instructions. Pick a specific point outside the bus and tell them all to gather there once they've left the bus.

Front door evacuations. For front door evacuations, instruct the students in the left front seat to exit first, followed by students in the right front seat. This alternating method will help you maintain an orderly evacuation and ensure that all students get off the bus. Exit in this way, from the front to the rear of the bus, until all students are off.

Rear door evacuations. For rear door evacuations, assign two of the older students to exit first and help the others out the door. Next, tell the students in the left rear seat to exit first, followed by students in the right rear seat. Again, continue alternating until all students are off the bus.

If possible, use both doors to evacuate your students as quickly as possible. In extreme emergencies, such as a rollover, you may need to use your bus's emergency windows or emergency roof exit.

Once the students are off the bus, make sure all are accounted for and that they stay well off the roadway.

Practicing evacuations

It's an excellent idea to practice these procedures with your students *before* you need to use them. Practicing an evacuation will help your students stay calm and follow your instructions if you ever need to conduct a real evacuation. Evacuation drills are required in some states or your company/school may have a policy on conducting mock evacuations.

Fires

A fire on your bus can be a scary thing, but again, your best course of action is to educate yourself about handling fires before you have to deal with one. This means knowing how to evaluate a fire quickly, knowing when and how to evacuate your bus, and knowing how to use a fire extinguisher.

Preventing fires

Even better than effectively fighting a fire is preventing one from occurring in the first place. Three of the common causes of vehicle fires are a failure in the electrical system, overheating of the brake system, and overheating of tires. On a school bus, you could also, unfortunately, encounter a fire in the passenger compartment caused by student vandalism or smoking.

The following procedures can help you prevent a fire on your bus:

- Regularly check the bus's electrical system, looking for frayed, worn, or broken wiring.

- Keep the bus clean of debris that could be flammable.

- Never use gasoline as a cleaning fluid for anything.

- Turn off your engine when fueling.

- Make sure defective fuses are replaced with fuses of the right size. Fuses that are too large could cause an overload and a fire.

- Check your batteries to make sure they are clean, covered, and the connections are tight.

- Prevent tire fires by checking pressure regularly.

- Do not operate a vehicle with hot tires. If there is visible smoldering, if you can smell burnt rubber, or if you can't hold the back of your hand against the tire, it's too hot.

- Prevent brake fires by not riding the brakes and making sure the brakes are fully released before driving.

- Watch your mirrors to spot smoke coming from tires or brakes.

- Keep an eye on your students. If you see lighters, matches, or suspicious behavior, pull your vehicle safely off the road and deal with the situation.

Evaluating the fire

When there is a fire on your bus, you will have to quickly answer two critical questions:

- Can I put out the fire myself?

- Do I need to evacuate the bus?

If the fire is small and not in the passenger compartment of the vehicle, you may be able to keep your students on the bus and put out the fire yourself with a fire extinguisher. Keep in mind, however, that many extinguishers will probably not be enough to handle any but the smallest of fires.

If the fire is large, or in the passenger compartment, pull your bus safely off the road and begin evacuation procedures. Get your students a safe distance from the bus and contact the fire department. Use a cell phone (if you have one), flag down another motorist, or — if you can't find anyone else to make the call — send two older, responsible students to a nearby house or business. *Stay with your students* — you are responsible for their continued safety.

Putting out fires

If the fire is small, you may try to put it out yourself with the fire extinguisher. Follow these steps for engine compartment and tire fires:

Engine compartment fires. If the fire is in the engine compartment:

- Get safely off the road and turn the engine off.

- Check for leaking fuel.

- If you suspect an electrical fire and you can safely do so, disconnect the battery cables.

- If you can safely open the hood, open it the minimal amount it takes to use the extinguisher on the fire. If there is any risk in opening the hood, you may be able to get some extinguishing agent on the fire by shooting up from underneath. If sand or dirt is available, you may use it when your extinguisher runs out.

- If you aren't able to completely put out the fire, evacuate your students and contact the fire department.

Tire fires. Hot gases of up to 1,000 degrees make putting out tire fires very difficult. The flames can come back over and over, so it's unlikely your extinguisher will have enough charge to stop a tire fire. If you have a tire fire:

- Sometime the best strategy is to keep driving until you reach a supply of water, as water is the most effective agent to use on tire fires. In other cases, it may be better to keep rolling for only a few minutes before coming to a stop.

- Do not pull into any area where the fire could endanger people or property.

- If your extinguisher empties, you may try throwing available sand, dirt, or snow on the tire.

- If you are not confident that the tire fire is 100 percent extinguished, evacuate the children and contact the fire department.

First Aid and First Aid Kits

Passenger illnesses, injuries, and accidents are other possibilities you should be prepared for. On a school bus, these can run the gamut from skinned knees and bloody noses, to broken bones, to life threatening injuries in a vehicle accident.

Hopefully your school district or company provides its school bus drivers training in first aid procedures and CPR. Nothing can replace hands-on training, but the following section will try to address some of the basics of first aid.

First aid kits

Your first aid kit will contain a lot of materials that can help you in a first aid situation. Be familiar with its contents and its location on your bus. Kit contents will vary, but they typically contain such items as:

- Bandages

- Splints

- Eye wash solution

- Gauze pads

- Compress dressings

- Instant ice packs

- Pain relief tablets

- Antiseptic sprays and burn gel

- Alcohol swabs

- Scissors and tweezers

- Adhesive tape

- Latex gloves

- Blankets

Make sure your first aid kit is fully stocked and that you replace items as needed.

Basic first aid principles

While many of the first aid situations you will encounter will involve little more than band-aids and wiping away tears, more serious injuries will require you to respond calmly and knowledgeably.

The following paragraphs talk about some basic first aid principles. Hopefully, they will reinforce training provided by your school or company.

When a student is injured, you should perform the following steps:

- Evaluate the situation

- Assess the condition of the student

- Notify emergency medical services

- Provide first aid as necessary

Evaluating the situation

When a first-aid situation arises, try to get an overall big picture of what has just taken place. This will give you a good indication of what you need to do next. If you cannot leave the injured student, send another passenger to get the first aid kit.

Assessing the condition of the student

Determine if the student is conscious, check the student's ABCs — the student's <u>a</u>irway, <u>b</u>reathing, and <u>c</u>irculation — and do a head-to-toe survey.

Check the victim's consciousness by tapping the student on the shoulder and shouting his/her name to see if you get a response.

To check the airway, look in the mouth for foreign objects. If there is something blocking the airway, try to remove it. Also see if the tongue is blocking the throat, as the tongue is quite often the source of the airway obstruction.

To check for breathing, turn your head and put your ear near the student's chest. Look at the victim's chest for movement and listen for any sounds of breathing. Put your face near the student's mouth to feel for breath on your cheek.

When checking for circulation, feel for a pulse at the carotid artery. To do this, place two or three fingers on the victim's adam's apple, and then slide the fingers just off to the side. The carotid artery is located in the grooved area just beside the adam's apple.

Do a head-to-toe survey to determine what injuries the victim has sustained. Start at the head and carefully examine the victim all the way down to his/her feet. Look for bleeding, protruding bones, any deformities, and medical alert tags, bracelets, or necklaces.

Notify emergency medical services

Contact emergency medical services directly on a cell phone, or radio your company/school. If a capable student is nearby, have him/her make the call so you can stay with the victim. If you are unable to call or radio, flag down (or have a responsible student flag down) a motorist. As a last resort, send a pair of responsible students to a nearby home or business to make the call.

Perform basic first aid

Ideally, first aid should be performed by someone trained in first aid procedures. If you are untrained, only perform actions that pose no risk of additional injury to the student, or actions absolutely necessary to save the victim's life.

Following are some very basic first aid guidelines for different injuries you may encounter:

Bleeding. To control bleeding, place a sterile gauze pad, bandages, or similar clean material over the wound. Apply direct pressure and elevate the wound above the level of the heart. (Do not elevate wounds, however, in cases of head, chest, or abdominal injuries.) If bleeding persists, add more gauze and continue to apply direct pressure. For cases of severe bleeding, you may need to apply pressure at a pressure point. This means pressing directly on the artery that is supplying blood to the injured area.

Shock. Shock occurs when the circulatory system fails to deliver oxygenated blood to all of the vital organs, especially the brain. Many injuries will involve some level of shock. You can prevent shock by having the victim lie down and elevating his/her legs 8 to 12 inches. (Do not elevate legs if there is a head, chest, abdomen, or spine injury.) Cover the victim with blankets or coats to help maintain the victim's normal body temperature.

Burns. Cover all burned skin that is blistered or charred with a dry sterile dressing or cloth. Elevate a burned arm or leg above the level of the heart to lessen pain and relieve shock.

Bone injuries. While open fractures are often obvious, closed fractures are harder to diagnose. Therefore, you should treat all suspected fractures as confirmed fractures. Fractures should be splinted to reduce pain and keep the fracture from worsening. To prevent further injury, splint the injured area in the position you find it. Use any rigid material you can find to splint the area and tie with strips of cloth, belts, rope, or similar material. Never tie the splint at the exact location of the injury and ensure that the ties do not cut off circulation.

Spinal injuries. If you suspect a spinal injury, immobilize the student's head — any movement could result in permanent paralysis. Place your hands on both sides of the head until medical help arrives. Hard or stiff objects can also be used to hold the victim's head still.

Bloodborne pathogens

If you administer first aid to a student, there is a chance you could be exposed to bloodborne pathogens. Bloodborne pathogens are microorganisms present in human blood that can cause disease. These include, but aren't limited to, the hepatitis B virus and the human immunodeficiency virus (HIV), the virus that causes AIDS.

Because you may respond in a first aid situation where there is blood or bodily fluids present, you should be aware of the *universal precautions* that exist to protect you from exposure.

Universal precautions include:

- Wearing impermeable gloves when touching body substances.

- Wearing any necessary personal protective equipment (such as gowns, gloves, masks, goggles, etc.)

- Performing proper clean-up with chemical germ killers (commercial germicide or bleach/water solution at 1:10 ratio).

- Using a mouth-to-mouth mask when performing CPR.

- Washing hands immediately after removing gloves or other protective equipment and after any hand contact with blood or potentially infectious fluids.

- Not bending, shearing, breaking, removing, or recapping any used needle or sharp. Dispose of used sharps in a proper container. These containers must be puncture resistant, properly labeled, and have leakproof sides and bottoms.

Talk to your company or school about their policies on handling bloodborne pathogens and any personal protective equipment they provide.

Driver _____

Instructor _____

Date _____

Location _____

Breakdowns and Accidents Review

1. What is a good reason for doing a pre-trip inspection?
   a. You may catch an unsafe condition before it causes an accident
   b. You can spot mechanical problems before they lead to breakdowns on the road
   c. Catching mechanical problems early will help your maintenance department control costs
   d. All of the above

2. Pre-trip inspections should:
   a. Be done every day
   b. Be done differently every time to make them more interesting
   c. Be done when it's convenient
   d. Only cover the engine components

3. If your bus breaks down, you should leave your students and walk to the nearest house or business to call your company.
   a. True
   b. False

4. When you are stopped on the side of the road because of a breakdown or accident, you should put out emergency warning devices to warn other drivers.
   a. True
   b. False

5. If you are in an accident, you should always evacuate the bus.
   a. True
   b. False

6. In an accident, which of these actions should be taken first?
   a. Fill out an accident report
   b. Treat the injured
   c. Get the bus safely off the road and set out warning devices
   d. Report the accident to your supervisor

7. If you need to evacuate the bus you should calmly give your students instructions and tell them where to gather once they've left the bus.
   a. True
   b. False

8. What is **not** a precaution you can take to prevent vehicle fires?
   a. Regularly checking the bus's electrical system to look for frayed, worn, or broken wiring
   b. Checking tire pressure regularly
   c. Making sure the brakes are fully released before driving
   d. Installing asbestos seats

9. When a passenger is hurt, you should assess his/her condition by checking the student's:
   a. Airway
   b. Breathing
   c. Circulation
   d. All of the above

10. When blood or bodily fluids are present, taking universal precautions can help you avoid exposure to the hepatitis B or HIV virus.
    a. True
    b. False

Extreme Weather

Safely driving a vehicle as large as a school bus is challenging enough, but add a heavy downpour, snowstorm, or dense fog, and your job becomes down right difficult.

But the fact is the weather, regardless of how severe it is, is rarely the direct cause of any accident. Accidents happen in bad (or extreme) weather because drivers fail to adjust their driving behavior to the current driving conditions.

Generally, the driving habits that are responsible for most extreme weather accidents include driving too fast for conditions, following too close (not leaving sufficient room between you and the vehicle(s) ahead of you), not adjusting to the reduced visibility caused by extreme weather, and driver inattention to the extreme weather conditions.

What lessons can we learn from this? While you can't control the weather, make sure you do control the three things you can, including:

1. Your vehicle (including the vehicle's speed)

2. Your following distance

3. Yourself

This chapter of your handbook will discuss how you can safely drive through the extreme weather conditions of snow, ice, rain, fog, and wind.

Snow

Snow, depending on the type and severity, can present a variety of dangerous conditions. Below you'll find a list of the different types of snow you'll encounter, and the appropriate driving technique for each:

- **Light snow.** Light, powdery snow presents few problems since it is quickly blown off the road surface. However if there is enough of this type of snow to cover the roadway, it will quickly form a slick, smooth surface from the weight of the traffic. When driving on such a surface, you should reduce your speed and increase your following distance. Determining the correct speed and safe following distance is up to your best judgement. But as a rule, following distance should be at least twice what it would be on a dry surface.

- **Heavy, wet snow.** Heavy, slushy snow can severely affect vehicle control. If wet snow becomes hard packed, it can cause an ice hazard on the road surface. Again, you need to reduce your speed and greatly increase your following distance.

- **Falling and blowing snow.** Falling or blowing snow can greatly reduce your visibility, making it hard to see the road, road markings, road signs, off ramps, etc. If you must drive in snowy conditions, reducing your speed and greatly increasing your following distance are the best techniques you can use to maintain vehicle control safety. If you must drive while it's snowing, you should also be aware of the dangers of a condition known as snow-hypnosis. Snow-hypnosis occurs when a driver is traveling directly into heavy snow and begins to focus on the falling snow instead of the road ahead. This can cause a hypnotic-like effect on the driver. The danger of snow hypnosis is especially prevalent at night or when you are fatigued.

In addition to the above, keep the following tips in mind when driving in snowy conditions:

Make sure your windshield wipers and defroster are working and in good order. These safety devices help you maintain proper visibility. Your windshield wiper blades should make full contact with your windshield and be free of icy build-up. If your blades are old and worn, get them replaced. Your defroster should blow a steady stream of warm air on your windshield and driver's side window. If the flow of air is weak, notify your supervisor or mechanic before heading out.

Avoid the use of high-beam headlights while driving in snowy conditions. The high shooting light will reflect off falling and blowing snow and back into your eyes, further reducing your visibility. Keep the light low and on the road.

Frequently clean your lights, reflectors, and other "visibility" safety devices. Ice, slush, and dirt on your lights and reflectors can greatly reduce their effectiveness, and can make your bus less noticeable.

Finally, keep in mind that when driving in or on snow, all slow maneuvers such as starting out, steering, backing, and turning should be done smoothly and with extreme care to minimize skids and slides.

In review, driving safely in or on snow requires:

- Gradually slowing down to maintain as much control over the vehicle as possible;

- Greatly increasing following distance;

- Making use of windshield wipers and defroster;

- Using low-beam headlights only;

- Understanding the dangers of snow-hypnosis;

- Cleaning snow and ice from lights and reflectors frequently; and

- Executing all slow maneuvers carefully and with great caution, and never attempting to pass.

Ice

You need to be aware of how icy conditions may affect your vehicle's traction. You also need to understand your vehicle. Knowing how to handle your vehicle and how it responds in various weather conditions is very important.

Ice is another extreme weather condition the professional school bus driver must be aware of. Remember, you don't have to live in the Great White North to encounter icy roads and bridges. In temperatures at or just above 32 degrees, a thin layer of water (even moisture from morning dew or frost) can turn to ice on a roadway, causing extremely dangerous driving conditions.

As with all extreme weather conditions, the safest techniques to employ are to reduce your speed and your increase following distance. But of these two, increasing your following distance is the most important. In addition, when driving on icy roads, you need to consider your stopping distance and be aware of the condition known as "black ice."

Stopping distance

Depending on the temperature and road conditions, stopping distance (distance needed to come to a safe and complete stop) on icy roads can increase four to ten times versus stopping from the same speed on a dry road.

On icy roads, keep a minimum of 6 to 8 seconds between you and the vehicle in front of you at speeds of 40 mph or less, and at least 8 to 10 seconds at speeds of 40 mph or more. In addition, steer, brake, and turn more slowly than normal. Doing so will help you prevent skids and slides.

Black ice

Black ice forms when temperatures drop rapidly and moisture on the road surface freezes into a smooth, almost transparent layer of ice on the road surface. What makes black ice particularly dangerous is that most drivers don't realize they are on it until it's too late. Black ice forms most typically on roadways that are not exposed to direct sunlight. Be cautious when driving on or into shaded areas, or roads around lakes and rivers.

Bridges and overpasses are especially susceptible to black ice. Black ice will tend to form first on bridges and overpasses because cold air circulates both above and below these structures, causing the temperature on them to drop more rapidly than on normal roads. Any moisture on the road surface of a bridge or overpass will freeze quicker and harder than elsewhere on the road. You need to exercise extreme caution and reduce your speed while traveling over bridges and overpasses.

Other tips

In addition to the above, you should keep in mind the following tips and suggestions for when you find yourself driving in icy conditions:

- Increase your visibility and chances of being seen by periodically cleaning your clearing your lights and reflectors of dirt, ice, and snow.

- Remember that posted speed limits are set for ideal weather and road conditions. Slow down when driving on ice.

- When driving uphill on icy roads, try to pick a path that will allow the most traction.

- To maintain control of your vehicle on curves and turns, reduce your speed prior to entering the curve or turn and use the brake sparingly. Any sudden acceleration or deceleration during a turn might send your bus into a skid.

- Avoid hard braking on icy roads.

To review, driving safely on icy roads requires:

- Reducing your speed in order to maintain as much control over your bus as possible;

- Never attempting to pass in icy conditions;

- Making all maneuvers such as turning, starting, and braking slowly and with great care;

- Greatly increasing your following distance (there should be a minimum of a 6-8 second cushion between you and the vehicle in front of you); and

- Being aware of the dangers of black ice, as well as the areas where black ice typically forms.

Rain

Rain presents three basic hazards for you as a professional school bus driver.

First, rain causes roadways to become slippery, especially when it first begins. All roadways are covered with a thin layer of oil, exhaust emissions, and other residues. When rain mixes with this layer, it results in an extremely slippery and dangerous road surface. This condition remains until additional rain can break down and wash away the oily mixture from the pavement. This process can take anywhere from a few minutes to several hours, depending on the severity of the rain.

To counter the effects of slippery roads caused by rain, you need to:

- Gradually reduce your speed; and

- Increase your following distance to compensate for the increased stopping distance you'll need — especially in emergency stopping situations.

Second, water on the road surface can also create the potential hazard of hydroplaning. Hydroplaning happens when a thin layer of water separates your vehicle's tires from the road surface. When a vehicle is hydroplaning, it is literally riding on a thin sheet of water.

When your tires are riding on water, they lose all traction and create an extremely dangerous driving situation. The faster you travel on standing water, the greater the chance of your vehicle hydroplaning. And no, size and weight do not matter. Any vehicle, if traveling fast enough, can hydroplane.

How can you avoid hydroplaning? There are two basic strategies for avoiding hydroplaning:

- Reducing your speed is the best and safest way to avoid hydroplaning. Remember, the heavier the rain, the slower your speed.

- Driving in the tracks of the vehicles directly ahead of you can help you avoid hydroplaning. Vehicles traveling ahead will throw water off the pavement and leave tracks. Driving in these tracks will give you the best possible traction under rainy conditions.

Third, rain also reduces your visibility. Rain, depending on how heavy it's pouring down, is difficult to see through and negatively affects your depth perception. In addition, rain will cause a constant film of water on your vehicle's windshield, further reducing your visibility. You need to make sure your windshield wipers and defroster are in good working order and use them when driving in rain. Doing so will help alleviate the reduced visibility.

To review, driving safely on wet roads requires:

- Gradually slowing down to compensate for slippery roadways and to reduce your risk of hydroplaning;

- Increasing your following distance to compensate for the added stopping distance;

- Driving in the tracks of other vehicles to further reduce your risk of hydroplaning; and

- Making use of windshield wipers and defrosters.

Fog

Fog greatly reduces your visibility and impairs your distance perception, making it perhaps the most dangerous type of all extreme weather conditions. Because of this, whenever possible you should avoid driving in foggy conditions. However, this is not always possible or practical.

The first rule of driving in fog is to never assume the depth or thickness of any fog. Fog can range from a momentary blurring of the windshield to being several miles thick. Slow your vehicle's speed. Reduction in your speed should be done gradually in order to avoid becoming a hazard for other motorists. Determining the correct and safe speed depends on the thickness of the fog and how greatly your visibility is reduced. You should never try to pass vehicles in these dangerous conditions.

When driving in fog, use low-beam headlights only. Low-beams serve two purposes:

- They help you see the immediate roadway; and

- They also allow other motorists to see you in the fog.

The use of high-beam headlights should be avoided in foggy conditions. The floating water particles that make up fog will reflect more light back in your eyes than on the roadway when high-beams are used, further reducing your visibility. When driving in fog, also take care that you do not out-drive your headlights — if you are not seeing objects in plenty of time to stop for them, you must reduce your speed.

As with rain, you need to make use of your windshield wipers and defroster when driving in fog. Driving in foggy conditions will cause a constant, fine mist of water on your vehicle's windshield, reducing visibility in the process. Using the windshield wipers and defroster will alleviate this condition.

To review, driving safely in fog requires:

- Not assuming the depth or thickness of the fog;

- Greatly reducing your speed;

- Using your low-beam headlights only;

- Using your windshield wipers and defroster;

- Avoiding passing in foggy conditions; and

- Not out-driving the vehicle's headlights.

Wind

The final extreme weather condition we'll discuss is high wind. Let's face it, your bus is not the most aerodynamically designed vehicle out on the road. Your bus is long, high, and solid. Because of this high profile, it can at times act like a sail — especially in high wind situations. In fact, if the wind blows hard enough, like a sudden and intense wind gust, a bus can be literally picked up off the ground and blown off the road.

Bottom line: drivers who are prepared for sudden and violent gusts of wind can better protect themselves, other motorists, and their passengers.

The effects of wind on a bus:

- Are more pronounced on a light vehicle than a heavy vehicle. Because of this, wind will affect your bus more when you are empty than when you have a full load of passengers.

- Can cause your vehicle to roll over or be blown off the road when the wind hits your bus from the side.

Guidelines for safe driving in windy conditions include:

- Reducing your speed — this will help you maintain control of your bus; and

- When you feel you are losing control of your bus, safely pulling off the road.

In Conclusion

You've noticed a couple of constant and very important themes throughout this chapter on driving in extreme weather conditions. They are so important in fact, that they deserve to be repeated here.

Remember, your best defense in any type of extreme weather is:

- Maintaining a safe following distance;

- Reducing your speed and adjusting it to the current weather conditions; and

- Controlling those things you can, including your following distance, your vehicle, and yourself.

Extreme Weather Review

1. What things do you most directly control while driving in severe weather?
   a. Your vehicle (speed)
   b. Your following distance
   c. Yourself
   d. All of the above

2. While driving in snow, driving maneuvers should be done quickly and with a lot of power to help you blast through drifting snow.
   a. True
   b. False

3. Snow-hypnosis can occur when:
   a. You're walking through a winter wonderland
   b. You're fatigued or driving at night
   c. You're driving directly into heavy snow and you begin to focus on the falling snow instead of the road
   d. Both b and c

4. Your vehicle's stopping distance can increase four to ten times on ice covered roads.
   a. True
   b. False

5. Which statement below is false concerning black ice:
   a. It forms when road surface temperatures drop rapidly
   b. Most drivers don't realize they're on it until it's too late
   c. It is a new licorice flavored frozen treat
   d. It is a thin, transparent layer of ice that develops most easily on shady roads, bridges, and overpasses

6. Since your bus is a large, heavy vehicle, you do not have to worry about the dangers of hydroplaning.
   a. True
   b. False

7. Fog is one of the most dangerous types of extreme weather because:
   a. It reduces your visibility
   b. It impairs your depth perception
   c. You cannot determine how thick or deep it is
   d. All of the above

8. You should use your low-beams in fog because:
   a. They help you see the immediate roadway
   b. They allow other motorist to more easily see you
   c. They use less electricity
   d. Both a and b

9. Because of the high profile of a school bus, it can be literally pushed over on its side if the wind is sudden and strong enough.
   a. True
   b. False

10. Maintaining a safe following distance and adjusting your speed to the current weather conditions are among your best defenses in extreme weather.
    a. True
    b. False

Compliance

As a school bus driver, there are many federal, state, and local requirements you must meet. The requirements were designed to ensure only safe and qualified drivers are entrusted with the transportation and safety of our school children.

This chapter will cover many of the requirements you must comply with. It will address the commercial driver's license requirements, drug and alcohol testing, driver qualifications, vehicle inspections, and hours of service.

Overview of the Federal Regulations

The Federal Motor Carrier Safety Regulations (FMCSRs) govern the safety and operations of commercial vehicles. School bus drivers are exempt from most of the FMCSRs when performing typical, day-to-day transportation of students. However, there are two notable exceptions: commercial driver's license (CDL) requirements and drug and alcohol testing. If your bus transports more than 15 passengers (including you), or weighs more than 26,001 pounds, you must have a CDL and comply with drug and alcohol testing requirements.

Under most circumstances, the rest of the rules you must follow are limited to state and local regulations. However, under certain circumstances you could be subject to federal requirements. You and your employer must comply with the federal safety regulations if:

- Your vehicle transports more than 15 passengers or weighs 10,001 pounds or more; AND

- Your employer is not a school district; AND

- You are not transporting students between their homes and school; AND

- You are crossing state lines.

Example: If you work for a bus company that contracts with a school district (rather than for a school district itself), and you drive a regular size school bus on an out-of-state field trip, you would have to comply with federal commercial vehicle regulations during that field trip.

If you fall under the federal requirements, you will have to be qualified according to the FMCSRs, do certain vehicle inspections, and follow the federal hours-of-service regulations. These topics will be covered in the later part of this chapter.

The CDL License

If your bus carries more than 15 passengers, you must have a CDL with a passenger endorsement. To get a CDL, you must pass a written knowledge test and a driving skill test. Many states will also require you to get a specific school bus endorsement on the license.

Your knowledge test will cover many of the basic principles of driving a commercial vehicle, such as shifting, backing, vehicle inspections, speed and space management, extreme driving conditions, and emergency maneuvers. The CDL test also has an air brake section. If you do not pass the air brake portion of the test, you will not be allowed to drive a vehicle with air brakes.

For your passenger endorsement, you will have to answer test questions on the loading and unloading of passengers, braking procedures, use of emergency exits and push-out windows, railroad crossing and drawbridge procedures, and responses to emergency situations such as unruly passengers or fires.

To receive the passenger endorsement, you must take your driving test in a passenger vehicle. The examiner will assess your skills in basic vehicle control, safe vehicle operations, and pre-trip inspections.

Notification responsibilities

When you have a CDL, there is certain information you are required to provide your employer. The information you must provide includes:

- You must provide 10 years of employment history when you are hired for a driving job;

- If your license is suspended, revoked, canceled, or you are disqualified from driving, you must tell your employer by the end of the business day following the day you are notified that you have lost your privilege to drive; and

- If you are convicted of a driving violation (other than a parking ticket) you must inform your employer in writing within 30 days of the conviction.

In addition to informing their employers, CDL drivers who are convicted of driving violations out of their home state must notify their licensing state of any conviction within 30 days.

Disqualifying offenses

CDL holders can be disqualified from driving for certain offenses. If you commit the following offenses in a commercial vehicle, you will be disqualified from driving:

- Driving under the influence of alcohol or a controlled substance

- Leaving the scene of an accident

- Committing a felony while in or using a commercial vehicle

- Violating an out-of-service order

- Committing certain railroad crossing violations

- Committing two or more serious traffic violations in a three-year period. (Serious traffic violations include excessive speeding, reckless driving, improper or erratic lane changes, following too closely, and any violation in connection with a fatal accident.)

If you commit a disqualifying offense, the length of time you are disqualified will depend on the seriousness of the offense and prior convictions. Disqualification periods for serious traffic offenses and railroad crossing violations are as little as 60 days; in contrast, drivers who use a commercial vehicle to commit a felony involving the manufacturing, distributing, or dispensing of illegal drugs will be disqualified for life.

Drug and Alcohol Testing

Drivers of commercial vehicles, including most school buses, must obey certain regulations pertaining to the use of illegal or dangerous drugs and the misuse of alcohol. The testing requirements do not exist because bus or truck drivers are more likely to use drugs or misuse alcohol — statistics actually show automobile drivers are much more likely to be under the influence of drugs or alcohol while behind the wheel than are commercial drivers. However, because commercial vehicles like your school bus are so large and could do so much damage if operated by an impaired driver, drivers are required to be tested to make sure they comply with the rules.

Testing is a *requirement* for driving a commercial vehicle. If you refuse to take an authorized drug or alcohol test, the consequences are the same as if you *failed* the test. You will not be allowed to drive, and, depending on your employer's policies, you could lose your job.

Drug and alcohol prohibitions

If your vehicle carries more than 15 passengers or weighs 26,001 pounds or more, federal regulations forbid you from:

- Driving with a blood alcohol concentration of .04 percent or greater;

- Using alcohol while driving or performing work duties;

- Using alcohol in the four hours before driving your school bus or performing work duties;

- Using alcohol for at least eight hours following an accident or until you take a post-accident alcohol test (if the situation requires you to be tested);

- Using drugs unless your doctor approves them and says they will not affect your ability to drive safely; and

- Refusing to take a required drug or alcohol test.

The drugs you will be tested for include narcotics (such as opiates, heroin, methadone, and morphine), marijuana, cocaine, phencyclidine (PCP), and amphetamines.

When alcohol tests are done, they will be conducted just before, just after, or while you are performing safety-sensitive work duties, such as driving.

Types of tests

There are six types of drug and/or alcohol tests you could be required to take. These include:

- Pre-employment tests

- Random tests

- Post-accident tests

- Reasonable suspicion tests

- Return-to-duty tests

- Follow-up tests

Pre-employment tests. All newly hired commercial drivers are required to take pre-employment drug tests when they are hired. Your company cannot allow you to drive until it receives a negative test result. Your new company is also required to ask your former employers about any drug or alcohol tests you failed or refused in the last two years.

At this time, a pre-employment alcohol test is not required.

Random tests. Once on the job, you could be picked for a random drug or alcohol test. Federal regulations require your employer to give random, unannounced drug and alcohol tests to a certain percentage of drivers each year. If you are with your company for a long time, there is a good chance that you will eventually be picked for a random test.

Post-accident tests. If you are in an accident, you could be required to take a post-accident test for drugs and alcohol. Post-accident tests are required in three circumstances:

• If there is a fatality in the accident;

• If someone is seriously injured in the accident (he/she requires medical treatment away from the scene) AND you receive a citation; or

• If a vehicle in the accident sustains disabling damage (it must be towed from the scene) AND you receive a citation.

Post-accident alcohol tests should be performed within two hours of the accident but can be administered up to eight hours after the accident if a more prompt test isn't possible. You are not allowed to consume alcohol for eight hours after the accident or until you take the test.

Post-accident drug tests must be taken within 32 hours after an accident.

If you are in an accident, keep in mind that post-accident tests often protect a driver's interests. If you were not under the influence of drugs or alcohol, a post-accident test result could exonerate you from any unfounded accusations.

Reasonable suspicion tests. If your supervisor has reason to think you may be using drugs or misusing alcohol, he/she could order you to take a reasonable suspicion test.

Your supervisor must base a reasonable suspicion test on specific observations and document why he/she thinks a reasonable suspicion test is warranted. Supervisors who order reasonable suspicion tests must be trained in recognizing the signs of drug and/or alcohol abuse.

Return-to-duty and follow-up tests. Return-to-duty and follow-up tests can be required of drivers who fail a drug or alcohol test. See the "Consequences of Failing or Refusing a Drug or Alcohol Test" section for more information.

Procedures for drug tests

Drug testing is performed on urine specimens. Specific regulatory procedures govern how testing must be done.

When you arrive at the collection site, you will be asked to provide identification and to remove unnecessary outer clothing. Generally, you will be given privacy to provide the specimen. If the collector believes you have tampered with the specimen, however, you may be asked to give another specimen under direct observation. A collection person of the same gender would observe the collection.

The urine specimen will be put in two containers that will be sealed and labeled in your presence. You will be asked to sign a testing form certifying you have not adulterated the sample and that you witnessed the sealing of the specimens.

The specimens are then sent to a laboratory where the main sample will be tested. After testing, the lab sends the test results to a medical review officer (MRO), a physician knowledgeable in drug abuse disorders. This MRO is responsible for reviewing the test results.

If the test is negative, the MRO will report the result back to your employer. If the test appears positive, the MRO will contact you to determine if there is a legitimate medical explanation (such as any prescription or over-the-counter drugs you may be taking) for the apparent positive test. The MRO will also inform you that you have 72 hours to request the second urine specimen be tested by an alternate lab if you believe the test result is an error. After the MRO's discussion with you (and review of the second lab's test results if a second test is requested), the MRO will report a verified negative or positive test result to your employer.

Procedures for alcohol tests

Alcohol tests are generally conducted on a breath testing device. Screening tests can be conducted using alternate methods, such as a saliva swab, but if a screening test shows a positive result, a breath testing device must be used for a confirmation test.

When you arrive for testing, you will be asked to provide identification and sign the testing form. If using a breath testing device, the testing technician will unwrap an individually-sealed mouthpiece, attach it to the testing device, and ask you to blow into the device for six seconds or until an adequate amount of breath is obtained.

If the alcohol test shows a blood alcohol concentration greater than .02, a confirmation test must be performed. If the confirmation test reveals the same result, you will not be allowed to drive and you may be subject to regulatory and company policy consequences.

Consequences for failing or refusing a drug or alcohol test

A driver who fails or refuses to take a drug or alcohol test cannot be allowed to drive or perform any job duties considered "safety-sensitive." Employers are required to provide drivers who fail or refuse a test with a list of resources, such as counselors or programs, that can help them deal with drug and/or alcohol problems.

Federal regulations do not require an employer to keep or fire a driver who fails a drug or alcohol test — this decision is made by the employer. However, if the company chooses to keep the driver, there are certain requirements that must be fulfilled.

If you fail or refuse a test, you must be evaluated by a person who works with people with drug and alcohol problems. This person will decide on a course of treatment or rehabilitation that you must complete before you can drive again. Once this person determines you've completed the treatment/rehabilitation, you must pass a return-to-duty test before you can drive again. After returning to the job, you will be given at least six unannounced follow-up tests in the next 12 months.

Exception. Drivers who have an alcohol test result showing a blood alcohol concentration of .02 percent or more, but less than .04 percent, must not drive for at least 24 hours, but are not subject to any other federal consequences. However, other state, school, or company consequences may apply.

Driver Qualifications

When your company or school hires you to drive a school bus, it must make sure you are qualified to do the job. Both the federal government and your state government have requirements you must meet to be considered "qualified." Undoubtedly, your school district or bus company will have their own requirements as well.

Some of the qualifications your employer will assess include:

- Your physical qualifications
- Your employment record
- Your driving record
- Any criminal history

Physical qualifications

Most states require school bus drivers to take some form of physical exam. The state (as well as your employer or school district) wants to make sure you do not have any physical or medical impairments that would prevent you from driving safely.

Passing a physical exam may be a condition of getting a school bus endorsement on your CDL in the state where you live. Or, it may be required before you take a job as a school bus driver. Most states also require you to be periodically re-examined and re-certified as fit to drive.

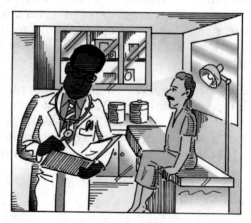

If you participate in operations that fall under federal requirements, you will have to be examined and certified according to federal regulations. Under federal regulations, you may not drive if you:

- Must take insulin to control diabetes;

- Have high blood pressure (161-180 systolic and/or 91-104 diastolic is considered marginal and you must be retested; blood pressure over 180 systolic and/or 104 diastolic will mean you are medically unqualified under federal rules);

- Do not have at least 20/40 vision in each eye with or without glasses or contact lenses;

- Have heart disease which causes you chest pain, fainting, or shortness of breath;

- Have respiratory problems, such as chronic asthma, emphysema, or chronic bronchitis;

- Have epilepsy;

- Are missing a foot, leg, hand, or arm;

- Have an impairment of the hand, finger, arm, foot, or leg that interferes with your ability to drive;

- Have poor hearing;

- Have a psychiatric disorder that is likely to interfere with your ability to drive the bus;

- Use amphetamines, narcotics, or other habit forming drugs; or

- Have a current diagnosis of alcoholism.

Federal regulations require drivers to be re-examined every two years.

Review of your employment record

When you take a job that requires a CDL, you must inform your new employer of all the commercial vehicle driving jobs you have held in the last 10 years. If your job duties make you subject to federal regulations, you must also inform a new employer of *all* your previous jobs for the last three years and your new employer must try to contact those former employers.

Your state, bus company, and/or school district may have additional policies about reviewing your employment record.

Review of your driving record

Your company or school district will almost certainly review your driving record before hiring you as a school bus driver. If your driving assignments make you subject to federal regulations, your employer must check your driving record for the last three years when you are hired, and once a year after you are hired.

Your employer will want to make sure you have a valid license and are not disqualified from driving. Your driving record must also pass muster against any state, bus company, or school district requirements where you are working.

Criminal background check

While there are no federal requirements on the issue, many, if not most, states have laws pertaining to criminal background checks for school bus drivers.

Some states require a criminal background check before they will issue a license endorsement for driving a school bus. In other states, the school district or bus company must do a check before hiring a driver. Your state law may require only that a check is made, or it may detail particular offenses — such as drug or sex crimes — that would disqualify a potential driver. Fingerprints are also required in some states.

Your school district or bus company may also have additional policies on criminal background checks.

Vehicle Inspections

Inspecting your vehicle as a part of your daily routine makes good sense. Regular inspections allow you to spot unsafe conditions or mechanical problems before they cause an accident or a breakdown on the road. See the "Vehicle Inspections" section in the Accidents and Breakdowns chapter for details on how to conduct an inspection.

Besides being just good practice, in many instances pre-trip and/or post-trip inspections are required by state regulations or your company's policy. Also, if you are involved in federally-regulated operations, you must do a pre-trip inspection and fill out a driver vehicle inspection report.

Pre-trip inspection

The federal regulations regarding pre-trip inspections are fairly brief, but important. Before driving your bus, the regulations require that you:

- Are satisfied that the vehicle is in safe operating condition;

- Are satisfied that the following parts and accessories are in good working order: service brakes, parking brake, steering mechanism, lighting devices and reflectors, tires, horn, windshield wipers, and rear vision mirrors;

- Review the last driver vehicle inspection report (DVIR); and

- If defects were noted on the DVIR, make sure all necessary repairs were performed and sign the report to acknowledge that the problems were corrected.

Driver vehicle inspection report

If you are driving your bus on a trip that falls under federal regulations, you must fill out a DVIR at the end of your work day. This DVIR must cover the vehicle's:

- Service brakes

- Parking brake

- Steering mechanism

- Lighting devices and reflectors

- Tires

- Horn

- Windshield wipers

- Rear vision mirrors

- Wheels and rims, and

- Emergency equipment

On the report, you must identify the vehicle and list any defect you found during your inspection(s) or during the course of operation that could affect the vehicle's safe operation or cause a breakdown. If you find no defects, your report this as well. You are required to sign the report and turn it into your company.

Any defect or deficiency you report on the DVIR must be corrected or your company must certify that correction is not necessary to safely operate the vehicle. This must be done before you drive the vehicle again.

Hours of Service

Federal hours-of-service regulations were designed to limit the number of hours a commercial driver may drive before obtaining rest. The goal is to keep tired drivers, who may present a risk to safety, off the road. Most states have adopted similar regulations for their commercial drivers, although school bus drivers are often exempt. Talk to your  supervisor about the state hours-of-service rules you may have to follow.

While the federal hours-of-service regulations are aimed more at truck drivers who often work long and irregular hours, you must also obey these rules if and when you fall under federal regulations.

There are three time rules you need to be aware of:

- The 10-hour driving rule;

- The 15-hour on-duty rule; and

- The 60/70-hour limits.

When you fall under federal regulations, you will also need to know how to fill out a record of duty status.

The 10-hour rule

All time spent behind the wheel is considered driving time. After 10 hours of driving time, you must have at least eight consecutive hours of rest before you can drive again.

The 15-hour rule

On-duty time includes all driving and work-related activities for your employer. Inspecting your bus, fueling, or practicing evacuation drills with your students would be examples of on-duty time. Also, any time you spend doing other compensated work for another employer is considered on-duty time.

After you have been on-duty for a total of 15 hours, you cannot drive again until you've had eight consecutive hours of rest.

The 60/70-hour limits

Your bus company must tell you if you should follow the 60-hour or 70-hour limit. Under the 60-hour limit, you can't drive after having been on-duty for 60 hours in seven consecutive days. Under the 70-hour limit, you can't drive after having been on-duty 70 hours in eight consecutive days.

Consecutive days does not mean a week (Sunday through Saturday) or "work week." It means any seven- or eight-consecutive-day period. You do not "start over" when counting total hours. The oldest day's hours drop out of consideration as each new day's hours are added.

Record of duty status

When you fall under federal regulations, you will be required to keep a record of duty status, commonly called a log.

The record of duty status contains a time-grid covering a 24-hour period. The grid is divided into four horizontal sections, with the labels:

- Off-duty

- Sleeper berth (sleeper berths are sleeping compartments commonly found in semi-trucks — you will probably never use this section of the grid)

- Driving

- On-duty (not driving)

You must draw lines in each section of the grid to correspond with your duty status throughout the day. Each time your duty status changes, you must bring your log up to date.

In addition to the grid, you must also record the following information on the record of duty status:

- Date
- Total miles driven today
- Vehicle number
- Name of your motor carrier
- Driver's signature
- 24-hour period starting time
- Main office address
- Remarks
- Name of co-driver (if applicable), and
- Total hours in each duty status

You must fill out your record of duty status in duplicate and submit the original to your employer within 13 days.

— Notes —

Driver _____

Instructor _____

Date _____

Location _____

Compliance Review

1. During day-to-day operations, most school bus drivers must obey:
    a. All federal commercial vehicle regulations
    b. All state regulations and local policies
    c. CDL requirements and drug and alcohol testing rules
    d. Both b and c

2. If you work for a company that contracts its services to a school district, you must follow federal regulations:
    a. When you cross state lines
    b. When you are not transporting students from home to school or school to home
    c. When you cross state lines AND you are not transporting students between school and home
    d. Every time you get in a school bus

3. To drive a bus that transports more than 15 passengers (including the driver), you must have a commercial driver's license.
    a. True
    b. False

4. Which of the following offenses will **not** cause you to lose your privilege to drive a school bus:
    a. Driving the bus under the influence of alcohol
    b. Committing a felony while driving the bus
    c. Making an improper right turn in the bus
    d. Leaving the scene of an accident involving your bus

5. If you refuse to take a drug or alcohol test, the consequences are the same as for failing the test.
    a. True
    b. False

6. You cannot drink alcohol in the four hours before you drive your school bus.
   a. True
   b. False

7. If you are picked for a random drug or alcohol test, your employer will give you three day's notice.
   a. True
   b. False

8. What are some of the things your employer might do to make sure you are qualified to drive a school bus?
   a. Require you to pass a physical exam
   b. Check your driving record
   c. Check to see if you have any criminal history
   d. All of the above

9. What is **not** a reason for doing a vehicle inspection?
   a. To check for mechanical problems that could lead to a breakdown or accident
   b. To comply with company or school policy
   c. To admire your bus's yellow paint
   d. To satisfy federal or state inspection requirements

10. The purpose of hours-of-service regulations is to make sure commercial drivers get adequate rest so they can safely drive their vehicles.
   a. True
   b. False

Personal Health Issues

There are many types of driving jobs — all of which present different health and safety obstacles for drivers. But regardless of the type of driving career, there is little doubt that a healthy, well-rested, and mentally alert driver is a safe driver — regardless of the vehicle being operated.

The personal health issues that will be covered in this chapter include:

- Fatigue management,

- Stress management,

- Diet and exercise, and

- Drivers, drugs, and drinking.

Fatigue Management

Driving while fatigued is a very dangerous driver condition and must be avoided at all times. Fatigue reduces your perception and reaction time, greatly impacts your ability to drive safely, and puts you and your passengers at unnecessary risk of injury or worse.

Just the facts

A quick review of fatigue-related accidents reveal the following statistics:

- About 56,000 fatigue-related transportation accidents occur each year.

- Fatigue is estimated to be a factor in 8 to 17 percent of all highway crashes.

- Fatigue is estimated to be a factor in 30 to 40 percent of large vehicle (bus and truck) crashes.

- Thirty-one percent of all fatal-to-the-driver crashes are considered to be fatigue related.

Studies conducted by the National Transportation Safety Board concluded that the most prevalent factors in fatigue-related large vehicle accidents are:

- The duration and quality of sleep during a driver's last sleep period.

- The amount of sleep the driver took in the previous 24 hours.

- Whether the sleep is continuous or interrupted.

Remember, nothing you do is worth getting hurt or hurting others over.

What is fatigue?

Fatigue (fuh-teeg') n. 1. A condition of weariness, exhaustion or tiredness caused by activity, exertion, or work. 2. Weakness caused by repeated stress. 3. The physical or mental condition of a **driver** who, because of exertion, stress, or lack of sleep, needs rest.

While all of the above definitions are relevant, this section will concentrate on number three. Fatigue is a generic term used in the transportation industry to describe any time a driver is sleepy, tired, exhausted (mentally or physically), and everything in between.

The two major causes of fatigue are lack of sleep (or loss of sleep — including quality of sleep and sleep debt), and working through or against the body's natural clock (called a circadian rhythm).

In addition to the above items (loss of sleep, quality of sleep, sleep debt, and circadian rhythms), this section will also discuss other fatigue-related items including signs of fatigue and tips for reducing the effects of fatigue.

Loss of sleep

Sleep is a lot like food and water — all three are necessary for human health and survival. Depriving your body of sleep is the same as starving or dehydrating yourself.

Generally speaking, most adults need between seven and eight hours of uninterrupted sleep within every 24-hour period in order to feel alert and well-rested. And although there are both "night owl" and "early bird" personalities out there, even these individuals need to recharge every day with a seven-to eight-hour uninterrupted rest period.

Recent sleep studies show a sleep loss of as little as two hours can affect alertness and performance including:

- Reduced judgement

- Slowed reaction time

- Lack of concentration

- Fixation

- Poor mood/attitude

Quality of sleep

The quality of your sleep is just as important as the amount. Uninterrupted is the key, but more on this issue later.

The fact remains that quality sleep is vital. Our health, well-being, and ability to do our jobs safely and successfully are strongly dependent on how well we meet our body's' need for rest and quality sleep.

Yet with the pressures of modern life, many people don't get sufficient quality sleep. Even if you get the requisite seven to eight hours of sleep each night, it may not be quality sleep.

So how can you get a good healthy night's sleep? While you may not be able to do much about the stress, anxiety, and overwork that can rob you of a good night's rest, there are steps you can take to help you get the quality sleep you need, including:

- **Getting plenty of regular exercise.** Something as simple as taking a brisk 20 to 30 minute walk a couple of hours before bedtime can help you achieve a deep, beneficial night's rest.

- **Taking a hot bath or shower just before bed.** Heat relaxes you muscles and helps prepare your body for sleep.

- **Avoiding eating a large meal before bed.** Don't eat a minimum of three hours before bedtime. The process of digestion can raise your metabolism and heart rate (two conditions that are not conducive to quality sleep), and lasts about three hours. If you feel the need to eat something, stay away from foods high in fats and sugar. Instead, try a banana or other healthy food.

- **Avoiding liquids.** Don't interrupt your beneficial sleep because of a full bladder.

- **Avoiding caffeine and nicotine before hitting the sack.** These are stimulants and can prevent you from falling asleep.

- **Avoiding alcohol late at night.** Remember, while alcohol may help you fall asleep, it will almost certainly cause you to wake up throughout the night.

- **Sticking to a routine.** Going to bed at night and waking up in the morning at around the same time each day can help you program your body's clock and sleep better.

- **Ensuring your sleep environment is quiet and comfortable.** If your room is too noisy, warm, or cold you will not get the proper rest you need. In addition, make sure your bed is properly supportive — not too firm or soft. Make sure your sleep environment is conducive to a good night's sleep.

- **Not forcing the issue.** If you find you just can't fall asleep, don't fight it. Get out of bed and find something relaxing to do. Read a book, play solitaire, etc., until your body is sufficiently relaxed enough to cause sleep.

Sleep debt

Sleep debt is just what the name implies. As stated previously, the average adult person needs between seven and eight hours of quality, uninterrupted sleep each day.

Occasionally, the person can function well on fewer hours of sleep. However, after a few days a "sleep debt" will develop.

For example, if you need eight hours of sleep to refresh and rejuvenate your mind and body, but only get six hours, you would have a two-hour sleep debt. If this behavior lasts for four days in a row, you would accumulate an eight-hour sleep debt. That's one full night's worth of sleep.

2 hours × 4 days = 8 hours (one night)

The longer you go without sleep, the more you will need to catch up, or pay your debt. However, the reverse is a myth — you cannot bank sleep. In other words, if you take a 10-hour rest break, you won't have a two-hour sleep savings account.

Circadian rhythms

In simple terms, a circadian rhythm is your body's internal or biological clock. Most people's internal clocks run on a 24-hour cycle with a couple of high points and low points during that time span.

Several time-related cues keep your body's clock set to your particular daily schedule. These cues can include sunlight and your work/rest schedule.

When your body's internal clock is moved to a different schedule (changing time zones, changing work shift — say first to third) your clock needs time to adjust to the new schedule. During the transition, the disruption to your internal clock can produce the same effects as sleep loss.

No matter when you work, or if you have a split-shift, or what sleep pattern you follow, most people's internal clock is set for two low points. The first is between 2 a.m. and 6 a.m. The second is between 1 p.m. and 5 p.m.

The afternoon low point is a prime driving time for school bus drivers taking their passengers from school to home. Signs that you're entering one of your low points include a lower body temperature, as well as changes in mood, motivation, and performance.

Signs of fatigue

The effects of fatigue are varied and serious. They include:

- Visual distortion (double and blurry vision)

- Reduced decision-making and problem-solving abilities

- Inhibited muscle response and coordination

- Reduced reaction time

- Inability to concentrate

- Irritability, exhaustion, or giddiness

- Erratic shifting, intermitent braking, and following vehicles too closely

- Highway hypnosis (driving without being aware of your surroundings)

Signs of fatigue are equally varied and serious. You and your passengers are simply too important to risk getting hurt by driving while fatigued. Signs of fatigue include:

- Eyes lose focus

- Frequent yawning

- Driving mistakes (missing an exit or turn)

- Loss of concentration (daydreaming)

- Experiencing highway hypnosis

- Drifting in your lane

- Loss of mental focus/ sharpness

- Eyelids feeling heavy

- Short-term memory loss (not remembering the last mile you drove)

- General lethargy

- 1-2 second blackouts (most dangerous sign)

If you are experiencing one or any combination of the above symptoms, it may be time to safely pull off the road and report your condition or get some needed rest.

Tips for reducing the effects of fatigue

Tips for reducing fatigue include:

- Light to moderate exercise (even a long walk will help). Exercise temporarily increases your heart rate and blood pressure and will energize your body.

- Eating a light, healthy meal consisting of fruit/vegetables for natural energy. Avoid that cheeseburger, fries, and chocolate malt for lunch just before your afternoon route. These types of food (heavy in saturated fat and sugar) will slow you and your body down and will increase fatigue.

- Avoid caffeine. Contrary to popular belief, caffeine is not a solution to fatigue. After the initial boost, the crash from caffeine will leave you even more tired.

- Get plenty of rest! This is the only sure way to prevent fatigue. Make sure you get plenty of quality, uninterrupted rest before reporting for work.

Stress Management

Stress is the body's reaction to the pressure, tension, or the constant change of everyday life. Stress is a physical or mental response to the events of everyday living. Stress causes the body to release chemicals into the bloodstream that set in motion a series of physical changes including:

- An accelerated heart and breathing rate;

- Higher blood pressure and blood sugar levels;

- Increased incidents of fatigue;

- Increased muscle tension; and/or

- Headaches, stomach disorders, and loss of concentration.

These changes are the body's defense mechanism for dealing with a stressful situation. While some stress is good, too much stress can lead to individual health problems, workplace injuries and accidents, and increased job dissatisfaction.

What causes stress?

Stress is a normal part of life and its causes, or *stressors*, are as varied as the people who suffer from stress — which is practically everyone. Stress can be caused by your job, family, financial situation, the weather, the news, or your favorite soap opera or sports team.

As stress continues, your body temporarily adjusts to the stress. If the causes of your stress are removed during this adjustment period, your body returns to normal. However, if stress goes on for a prolonged period of time, your body will fail to adjust and will wear out, weakening your body's natural defenses to disease. Stress can even lead to burnout.

From a medical standpoint, stress can cause high blood pressure, pain, breathing difficulty, digestive disorders, insomnia, and fatigue. Psychologically, stress can cause frustration, irritability, anger, impatience, worry, a lack of self confidence, poor listening, and alcohol/drug abuse.

Stress can also negatively affect your job performance. Stress can cause you to rush, become easily angry, and cause accidents.

Dealing with stress

Because of what you do and who you are transporting, safety needs to be your top priority. You simply cannot allow stress to interfere with your safe job performance.

Awareness is the first step in managing your stress. Watch for the warning signs of stress. You can manage stress by using one or more of the following stress-reduction techniques:

- Take short breaks — relax during these breaks

- Exercise. Taking a short, brisk walk or jog will help you work out your stress

- Get plenty of quality rest

- Start or maintain healthy eating habits

- Learn and practice stress-relieving techniques such as deep breathing

- Manage your time better — set reasonable priorities and schedules

- Release your tension by laughing or crying — whatever the case may be

- Share your stress with others — talk to a friend, co-worker, or supervisor

Diet and Exercise

A proper diet and light to moderate exercise are two ways you can maintain your health, manage fatigue, and reduce stress. A healthy diet and right amount of exercise can also help you work safely and productively and feel your best.

The five basic food groups

A healthy diet means choosing grain products, vegetables, fruits, low fat milk products, lean meats, fish, poultry, and dry beans. You should limit the number of fats and sweets you eat.

Foods contain combinations of nutrients and other healthful substances. To make sure you get all of the nutrients and other substances you need to remain healthy, the U.S. Department of Agriculture (USDA) recommends you choose a recommended number of daily servings from each of the five food groups.

Group	Number of Servings
Grain Products	6 to 11
Vegetable	3 to 5
Fruit	2 to 4
Milk	2 to 3
Meat and Beans	2 to 3

Foods that provide few nutrients and are high in fat and sugars should be chosen sparingly.

What is a serving?

So, what is a serving? The table below gives some examples. As you view the table, notice that some of the serving sizes may be smaller than what you may usually eat. For example, if your lunchtime sandwich includes two slices of bread, that counts for two servings.

Group	What Counts as a Serving
Grain Products	1 slice of bread 1 ounce of ready-to-eat cereal 1/2 cup of cooked cereal, rice, or pasta
Vegetable	1 cup of raw leafy vegetables 1/2 cup of other vegetables (cooked or chopped raw) 3/4 cup of vegetable juice
Fruit	1 medium apple, banana, or orange 1/2 cup of chopped, cooked, or canned fruit 3/4 cup of fruit juice
Milk	1 cup of milk or yogurt 1 1/2 ounces of natural cheese 2 ounces of processed cheese
Meat and Beans	2-3 ounces of cooked lean meat, poultry, or fish 1/2 cup of cooked dry beans 1 egg 2 tablespoons of peanut butter 1/3 cup of nuts

Some foods fit into more than one group. Dry beans can be counted as servings in either the meat and beans or vegetable group, but not in both groups.

A healthy diet and you

Hours behind the wheel, performing many stops in a short amount of time, and waiting to go on duty between shifts can lead many bus drivers to choose snacking (junk food) over regular, healthy meals as a way of passing the time and getting through the day. Yet in the end, we are what we eat.

Today, nutritional science is discovering that the food we eat plays a major role in virtually all aspects of our lives — from our emotional stability to our energy level to our overall health and well-being.

While snacking has been identified as the leading cause of obesity, it can also be beneficial if done properly and with the right foods. For instance:

- Replace potato chips with carrot chips. Carrots are a great source of carotene — a natural calorie cluster buster that also speeds the body's metabolism.

- Replace french fries with celery sticks. Celery is loaded with minerals that help energize the glandular system producing weight-gain-deflecting hormones.

- Replace cookies, donuts, and cake foods with melon slices. Melons are a high-energy food loaded with vitamin C.

- Replace candy and high-sugar foods with apples, bananas or dried fruit. These are good alternatives to sweets, keep well, and can limit the amount of fat and calories the body's fat cells absorb.

Don't cut out the rough stuff

Fiber is essential to maintaining good health. Fiber, or roughage, is the indigestible component of grains, fruits, and vegetables.

There are basically two types of fiber — soluble and insoluble. Soluble fiber, as found in oats, beans, and many fruits, can help lower cholesterol and can stabilize blood sugar.

Insoluble fiber, like that found in corn, wheat bran, and leafy and root vegetables, can help prevent constipation and lower the risk of colon cancer.

There are plenty of excellent ways to increase your fiber intake. Such as:

- Replacing processed cereals and white bread with whole grain breads and cereals, rice, and pastas;

- Leaving the (washed) peels and skins on fruit and vegetables when eating them. These are great sources of dietary fiber;

- Having a whole orange or grapefruit instead of juice for breakfast or anytime of day; and

- Increasing water intake to help fiber do its job.

Exercise

A growing concern for many bus drivers today is that of personal health and fitness. And there is good reason for this concern.

Because of the sedentary work-life of a typical school bus driver, many don't get the exercise their bodies need. Throw into this work-life irregular eating habits, tight schedules followed by prolonged down time, and it is easy to understand why many bus drivers have a tough time staying fit.

However, as medical science further examines the importance of regular exercise, the list of its benefits continues to grow — everything from reduced stress to weight loss to increased energy to a healthier mind and body.

When most people think of exercise, they think of working out at a gym or health club. In reality, any type of low to moderate activity can help improve your total well-being. The USDA recommends 30 minutes of physical activity on most (preferably all) days of the week.

There are few legitimate reasons not to exercise regularly — even for school bus drivers who may have rationalized not exercising with excuses such as, "There simply isn't enough time in the day," or "My work schedule doesn't allow for regular exercise."

The following is a list of simple yet effective exercises that can be done almost anywhere, any time.

For the back, neck, and shoulders

- **Crunches.** These require little space and can be done just about anywhere. Lying on your back, cross your arms across your chest so that your right hand is touching your left shoulder and your left hand is touching your right. Now, keeping your head straight, lift your shoulders 6-8 inches off the floor. Return slowly and repeat. Do as many as you feel comfortable with. Crunches are great for strengthening your lower back and abdominal muscles.

- **Knees to chest.** Again, lying on your back, bring your left knee up to your chest and hold it with you hands for five to 10 seconds. Repeat with your right knee. This is good for stretching and strengthening back and buttocks muscles.

The below exercises are designed to strengthen your neck, shoulders, and upper back muscles and can be done while sitting behind the wheel or wherever convenient.

- **Shoulder rolls.** Roll your shoulders up, backwards and down as far as you can comfortably move them. Repeat 10-12 times, then reverse you direction.

- **Shoulder extension.** Bring your shoulders up and backwards to their fullest extent. Hold this position for five to 10 seconds while tightening your upper back and neck muscles. Repeat three to five times.

- **Neck rotations.** Turn your neck one direction to its maximum extension and hold this position for five seconds. Do the same in the opposite direction, then repeat three to five times.

- **Neck side bends.** Keeping your head forward, bend your neck to one side and then the other, trying to touch your ear to your shoulder each time. Repeat three to five times.

Repeat these exercises three or four times per day or as often as you feel comfortable with. They are quick and easy and excellent for beginners.

For the whole body

While exercises to tone specific body parts are great, you also want to do some overall exercise to get your heart pumping and blood moving. Even ordinary household activities can qualify as whole body exercise. Get your body moving by choosing one (or more) of the following activities:

- Conditioning or general calisthenics

- Cycling (stationary or on the road)

- General house care/cleaning

- Mowing the lawn or any type of outside maintenance/rec-reation/gardening

- Walking — walking is an effective low impact exercise that is easy on the ankles, knees, and hips

Drivers, drugs, and drinking

One in 10 Americans has a drug or alcohol problem. And no profession or industry is immune from this problem. The consequences of driving while under the influence are very serious — especially when you consider the cargo you're transporting.

As well as being illegal, a bus driver under the influence of drugs or alcohol is dangerous to himself/herself, his or her passengers, and other motorists. In the Compliance chapter, we talked about the required testing for drug use and alcohol misuse for bus drivers. In this next section, we'll address these issues from the perspective of your own personal health and the safety of you and your passengers.

Alcohol abuse

Alcohol is a socially accept-able drug that when con-sumed in moderation, is considered a recreational bev-erage. However, when con-sumed primarily for its physical and mood-altering effects, it is considered sub-stance abuse.

Signs of use include lack of coordination, slowed reaction rate, slurred speech, dulled mental processes, and odor of alcohol on breath.

The chronic consumption of alcohol is defined as an average of three or more servings a day of beer (12 ounces), whisky (1 ounce), or wine (6 ounces). Chronic consumption of alcohol over time may result in the following health hazards:

- Dependency on alcohol

- Fatal liver diseases

- Kidney disease

- Pancreatitis

- Ulcers

- Birth defects

Marijuana

Marijuana is used as a mild tranquilizer, altering the user's mood and perception. Marijuana depresses the central nervous system's reactions. It affects the brain, altering the proper interpretation of messages.

The signs of use include slowed speech, reddened eyes, a distinctive odor (similar to a combination of sweet alfalfa and incense) on clothing, chronic fatigue, irritating cough, sore throat, and a lackadaisical attitude.

Marijuana use can cause several serious health conditions. One marijuana cigarette (joint) contains the same amount of cancer causing substances as one-half to one pack of cigarettes. It also irritates the lungs. Chronic smoking can cause emphysema-like conditions.

One joint causes the heart to race and be overworked. People with undiagnosed heart conditions are at risk.

Regular use can affect mental functions, including:

- Impaired short-term learning

- Diminished concentration

- Impaired signal detection

- Impaired visual distance measurements

- Erratic cognitive function

- Delayed decision making

- Distortion in time estimation

Cocaine

Cocaine is a powerful physical and mental stimulant that energizes the entire central nervous system. Use causes muscles to become more tense, the heart to beat faster and stronger, and the body to burn more energy. The brain experiences an exhilaration caused by a large release of neurohormones associated with mood elevation.

Signs of use include wide mood swings, difficulty concentrating, restlessness, hallucinations, paranoia, insomnia, dilated pupils and visual impairment, profuse sweating and dry mouth, high blood pressure, heart palpitations, and irregular heart rhythm

Cocaine causes the heart to beat faster and harder. It rapidly increases blood pressure. Cocaine causes spasms of blood vessels in the brain and heart, which can lead to ruptured vessels causing strokes and heart attacks.

Strong psychological dependency can occur within a short period of time. Cocaine causes the strongest mental dependency of any known drug. Treatment success rates are lower for cocaine than any other chemical dependency.

Opiates

Opiates are narcotic drugs that alleviate pain. They depress body functions and reactions. When taken in large doses, opiates cause a strong euphoric feeling.

Signs of use include mood changes, depression and apathy, impaired coordination, constricted pupils, and physical fatigue and drowsiness.

Narcotics increase pain tolerance. Because of this, someone who is under the effects of an opiate could injure himself/herself and not seek medical attention because he/she is not experiencing a great deal of pain.

The effects of narcotics are multiplied when used with other depressant drugs and alcohol, causing an increased risk of an overdose.

Amphetamines

Amphetamines are central nervous system stimulants that speed up both the mind and body. Low doses give the user a physical sense of energy. Higher doses cause mental exhilaration. Legal use of amphetamines is limited to an extremely narrow range of medical conditions.

Signs of use include increased heart rate and blood pressure, heart palpitations and irregular heartbeat, rapid respiration, profuse sweating, restlessness, hyperexcitability, and inability to concentrate.

Regular amphetamine use produces high psychological dependence on the drug. It also increases tolerance to the drug.

Amphetamines can cause heart and brain damage caused by a heart attack or stroke. The stimulation caused by the drug can also cause the user to be impulsive and lash out with bizarre and violent acts.

Phencyclidine (PCP)

Phencyclidine (PCP) acts as a depressant and a hallucinogen, and sometimes as a stimulant. In low doses it produces sedation and euphoric mood changes. Larger doses can produce a coma-like condition with muscle rigidity and a blank stare with the eyelids half closed.

Signs of use include severe confusion and agitation, extreme mood shifts, impaired coordination, muscle rigidity, jerky eye movements, dilated pupils, profuse sweating, dizziness, and rapid heartbeat.

The possibility of accidents and overdose with the use of PCP is high. This is due to the extreme mental effects of the drug combined with its anesthetic effect on the body.

PCP use can cause irreversible memory loss, personality changes, and thought disorders.

Driver _____

Instructor _____

Date _____

Location _____

Personal Health Issues Review

1. Which of the following are **not** effects of fatigue?
   a. Double and/or blurry vision
   b. Inhibited muscle response and coordination
   c. Irritability, exhaustion, and giddiness
   d. Low nutritional value

2. Signs of fatigue include:
   a. Drifting into other lanes
   b. Short-term memory loss
   c. Inability to concentrate
   d. All of the above

3. Ways to fight fatigue include:
   a. Getting a solid eight hours of sleep
   b. Establishing a regular schedule/routine
   c. Avoiding driving during your body's "down time"
   d. All of the above

4. Exercise, proper rest, and healthy eating habits are all ways to reduce stress.
   a. True
   b. False

5. A healthy diet means choosing:
   a. Grain and low-fat milk products
   b. Vegetables and fruits
   c. Lean meats, fish, and poultry
   d. All of the above

6. The USDA recommends 30 minutes of physical activity on most days.
   a. True
   b. False

7. Walking is not an effective form of exercise.
   a. True
   b. False

8. Which is **not** a risk associated with chronic consumption of alcohol?
   a. Liver disease
   b. Kidney disease
   c. Acne
   d. Birth defects

9. Chronic consumption of alcohol is defined as any use of alcohol.
   a. True
   b. False

10. The use of marijuana, cocaine, amphetamines, phencyclidine, or any illegal drug can cause serious health problems.
    a. True
    b. False

— Notes —

— Notes —

— Notes —

— Notes —

— Notes —

— Notes —

— Notes —

— Notes —